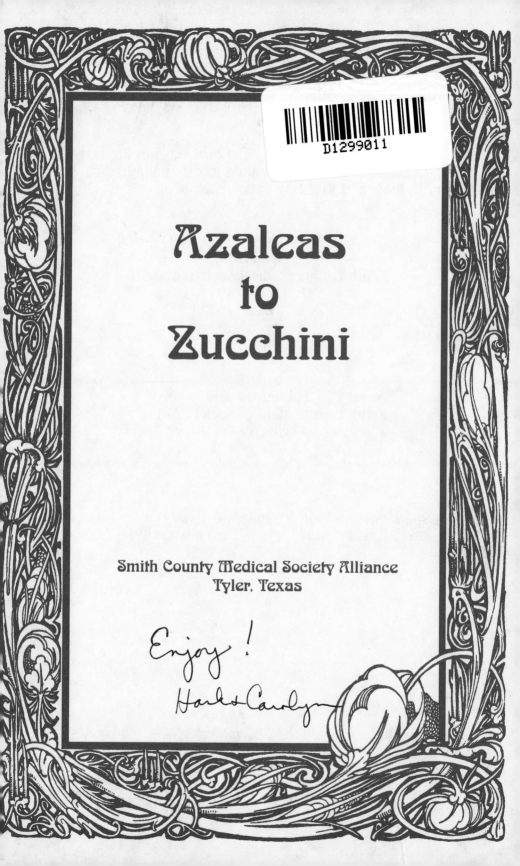

Azaleas
to
Zucchini

Smith County Medical Society Alliance
Tyler, Texas

Enjoy !

Hank & Carolyn

by
Smith County Medical Society Alliance

Additional copies of *Azaleas to Zucchini* may be obtained at the cost of $15.95, plus $2.75 postage and handling, each book. Texas residents add $1.24 sales tax, each book.

Send to:
Smith County Medical Society Alliance
P.O. Box 7491
Tyler, Texas 75711

ISBN: 0-9648536-0-4
First Printing   November, 1995

Printed in the USA by

WIMMER
The Wimmer Companies, Inc.
Memphis

INTRODUCTION

East Texas. A region immersed in scenic beauty and tradition. From the majestic pine trees and clear lakes to the grand pageantry of azaleas and roses.

People here are entwined in the celebration of life. It is reflected in our lifestyles and heritage of fine foods. It is cultivated through the host of festivals and other forms of entertainment unique to East Texas.

Join us in our celebration through the pages of this cookbook. Savor the delicious recipes and experience festivals and entertainment steeped in East Texas tradition.

The *Azaleas To Zucchini* Committee wishes to express heartfelt thanks to countless individuals for their generous contributions of recipes, testing, editing and marketing. It is impossible to thank our numerous friends individually, but we are deeply grateful to them and to our entire Smith County Medical Society Alliance for their help and support. We hope you share our pride in this cookbook which is a reflection of our East Texas heritage and lifestyle.

Cover and Design by Graydon R. Parrish and Michael W. Gottlieb. Raised in Tyler, Texas, Graydon Parrish is a professional fine artist painting in the classical style. Presently, Graydon resides in Massachusetts where he maintains a studio and is attending Amherst College. His art is represented by Roughton Galleries in Dallas. A close friend of Graydon's, Michael Gottlieb is the Associate Promotion Art Director for *Good Housekeeping Magazine* and a freelance graphic designer. Michael has designed for Sony Music Entertainment, *Country Living Magazine*, and the Intercontinental Hotel chain. He lives and works in New York City.

COOKBOOK COMMITTEE

Chairmen:

Joyce Hudnall
Joey Roberts
Betty Robinson

Committee:

Carole Jean Abernathy
Barbara Anderson
Kristi Armstrong
Dianna Brown
Susan Donaldson
Maytee Fisch
Carol Foox
Donna Freeman
Mayra Gallardo
Carole Haberle

Marsha Harrison
June Hillis
Ethel Knarr
Ali Langsjoen
Joan LeSauvage
Junella McClusky
Sharon Nelson
Karen Norton
Alice Parrish
Sandie Propst
Rhonda Reuter

Ann Robertson
Lynne Short
Jill Sigal
Betty Ann Smith
Mary Gean Smyth
Elizabeth Snider
Kathy Spivey
Marie Starling
Mary Lou Tyer
Martha Walker

Alliance Presidents 1991-1995:

Marsha Harrison
Helen Israel

Kay Scroggins
Alice Parrish

D'Anna Wick

ACKNOWLEDGEMENTS

Azaleas To Zucchini is the result of several years of work by a dedicated committee. It represents a labor of love that could never have been realized without the generous financial support of the following:

- East Texas Medical Center
- Mother Frances Hospital
- Smith County Medical Society
- University of Texas Health Center at Tyler

TABLE OF CONTENTS

THE SMITH COUNTY MEDICAL SOCIETY ALLIANCE

In 1934, East Texas was experiencing a major oil boom. It couldn't have come at a better time! Our nation was struggling to recover from the Great Depression. President Franklin Roosevelt, attempting to rally people to live in hope again, had just reassured them, "The only thing we have to fear is fear itself".

Also in 1934, thirteen courageous and hopeful physicians' wives united to become charter members of the Smith County Medical Society Auxiliary. Their goal was to work in community service in areas such as health, education, and philanthropy. Today, 275 physicians' wives are members of a newly-named Smith County Medical Society Alliance which grew from that early organization. We are continuing to work to improve the quality of life for all citizens as we give unselfishly to projects such as CPR certification, car safety seat programs, the war on drugs, Youth Yellow Pages, Parents Anonymous, conferences on violence in the community, Child Lures, Distinguished Lecture Series at the University of Texas at Tyler, Health Fair, free immunizations through "Shots Across Texas", putting *The Little Peoples' Guide To The Big World* in school libraries, and providing Hard Hats for Little Heads, bicycle helmets for children.

Our biggest semi-annual project is the Book Fair sale which benefits local nursing and medical-related career students. Over $200,000 has been awarded since its inception in 1969. We also give Presidential Scholarships at our branch of the University of Texas and at Tyler Junior College.

The publication of *Azaleas To Zucchini* is our newest effort to provide the ways and means by which we can continue our sixty-one year old tradition of service and help to all who live in beautiful East Texas.

Appetizers and Beverages

Tyler Azalea and Spring Flower Trail

Celebrate spring as Tyler is transformed into a showcase of natural beauty. The Azalea Trail encompasses several miles of brilliant azaleas, beautiful dogwoods, spring flowers and historic homes.

The city of Tyler celebrates with a profusion of special events. Highlights include the Azalea Trail 10K and Fun Run and the mesmerizing sounds of the Tyler Jazz Celebration.

ARTICHOKE DIP

1 can artichoke hearts,
    drained and crushed
1 cup Hellmann's
    mayonnaise

½ cup grated Parmesan
    cheese
½ teaspoon garlic salt
pepper to taste
paprika

Preheat oven to 350 degrees. Combine all ingredients except paprika, mixing well. Turn out into a prepared baking dish, sprinkle paprika on top for color, and bake for ½ hour.

BASIL PESTO

2 cups lightly packed fresh
    basil leaves
½ cup lightly packed fresh
    parsley leaves
½ cup olive oil
3 tablespoons pine nuts

2 garlic cloves, peeled and
    sliced
½ cup freshly grated
    Parmesan cheese
2 tablespoons very soft
    unsalted butter
salt to taste

In food processor or blender, puree basil, parsley, olive oil, pine nuts and garlic. Stir in Parmesan cheese and butter by hand. Season to taste with salt. If pesto is too thick, just before serving add a spoonful or two of warm cooking oil. Use for goat cheese and sun-dried tomato torte, chicken or vegetable soup, pasta, salads or dips. Yields 1¼ cups.

Pesto idea - Top slices of French bread with cream cheese, pesto and sun-dried tomatoes. Heat at 450 degrees for 5 minutes. Serve as appetizers.

Azaleas were first introduced to Tyler in 1929 by Maurice Shamburger, one of the city's early nurserymen. After a test garden yielded abundant blooms, he had the colorful plants shipped to Tyler by boxcar load from Georgia. The Spring Azalea Trail encompasses 120 home gardens and attracts more than 100,000 visitors a year.

HOT BEAN DIP

1 can refried beans
8 ounces cream cheese
8 ounces sour cream
1 package of taco seasoning

1 bunch of green onions,
chopped
1 clove of garlic, minced
1 cup grated Cheddar cheese

Combine all ingredients except Cheddar cheese. Bake at 350 degrees until hot. Top with grated Cheddar cheese. Heat until cheese is melted.

BASIL PARMESAN LOAF

8 ounces cream cheese,
softened
4 ounces goat cheese
1 cup loosely packed spinach
leaves, rinsed and dried
¾ loosely packed fresh
Italian (flat-leafed)
parsley
¼ cup loosely packed fresh
basil leaves

1 teaspoon garlic, minced
¼ cup vegetable oil
¼ cup walnuts, finely
chopped
1 cup freshly grated
Parmesan cheese
¼ cup slivered sun-dried
tomatoes

Combine cream cheese and goat cheese in a bowl and mix until smooth. Set aside. Combine spinach, parsley, basil and garlic in bowl of a food processor. With motor running, slowly drizzle the oil over mixture through the feed take; continue processing until smooth. Transfer mixture to a bowl, add walnuts and Parmesan cheese and mix thoroughly. Line a 5½ x 2½-inch loaf pan with plastic wrap, leaving extra wrap hanging over the sides. Spread ⅓ of the cheese mixture evenly over the bottom of the pan. Next, spread half the pesto mixture, and arrange a layer of sun-dried tomatoes on top. Repeat the cheese, pesto, and tomato layers. Finish with the remaining third of the cheese mixture. Cover with overhanging plastic wrap, and refrigerate for 24 hours. To serve, allow loaf to come to room temperature, about 30 minutes. Invert onto a platter and provide a cheese slicing knife. Serve with crackers and/or bread.

HOT BROCCOLI DIP

1 medium yellow onion,
 chopped
½ cup celery, chopped
2 teaspoons margarine
2 10-ounce packages of
 chopped frozen broccoli
 (or spinach)

1 medium can of drained
 sliced mushrooms
2 6-ounce rolls of garlic
 cheese
1 can mushroom soup
salt and pepper to taste
dash celery salt

Sauté onion and celery in margarine. Cook broccoli (or spinach) and drain well. Add mushrooms, onion and celery mixture to broccoli (or spinach). Add cheese that has been cut into pieces. Then add mushroom soup to mixture and heat. Serve with corn chips or raw assorted vegetables.

HOT NOONDAY ONION DIP

1 cup mayonnaise
1 cup Swiss cheese, grated
1 cup sweet Noonday onion

1 tablespoon fresh lemon
 juice
4-5 drops Tabasco
salt to taste

Preheat oven to 325 degrees. Grate onion or put in food processor. Put in another bowl and mix with all other ingredients. Place in small baking and serving dish. Bake 15 minutes or until bubbly. Brown top under broiler 2 minutes, watching carefully. Serve with toast points or crackers. Yields 2 cups.

CURRIED CHICKEN BALLS

8 ounces cream cheese,
 softened
4 tablespoons mayonnaise
1½ cups chopped almonds
1 tablespoon butter
2 cups of cooked chicken
 breast, chopped

3 tablespoons chutney
1 teaspoon salt
2 teaspoons curry powder
1 cup grated coconut, toasted
 optional

Blend cream cheese and mayonnaise. Sauté almonds in butter until lightly browned. Add almonds, chicken, chutney, salt and curry powder to cream cheese mixture. Shape into walnut size balls and roll in coconut if desired. Chill until ready to serve. Yields 5 dozen balls.

CHUNKY CHEESE SPREAD

2 cups shredded Cheddar
  cheese
2 cups pecans, toasted and
  chopped
8 to 10 green onions, chopped
  finely

1 teaspoon mayonnaise to
  moisten
1 8-ounce jar jalapeño jelly or
  jelly of your choice

Mix cheese, pecans, chopped onions and mayonnaise together. Spread in glass pie plate, quiche dish or flan pan. Let stand in refrigerator at least 2 hours or overnight. When ready to serve, cover top with jalapeño jelly. Serve with crackers. Keeps well in refrigerator 2 to 3 days. Note: Due to amount of mayonnaise, this spoons onto crackers easier than spreading with knife. Serves 10-12.

CURRIED APPLE DIP

1 15-ounce jar applesauce
1 cup sour cream

1 envelope dry onion soup
  mix
1 teaspoon curry powder

Combine ingredients and chill. Excellent dip for cold shrimp or other seafood. Also tasty with crudités or crackers.

CHILI CHEESE ROLL

1 pound Velveeta cheese
½ pound Cheddar cheese
2 or 3 cloves garlic, finely
  chopped

1 cup pecans, toasted and
  finely chopped
chili powder
paprika

Soften or melt cheeses in dish in 275 degree oven for ½ hour. Combine garlic and nuts with soft cheese and blend thoroughly. Form 2 long rolls and roll in chili powder and paprika. Wrap and store in refrigerator. Use as a spread on crackers. Serves 15.

CHEESE BREAD CUBES

1 loaf unsliced day-old bread
½ cup butter
1 cup grated cheese

1 3-ounce package cream
  cheese
2 egg whites (beaten stiff,
  not dry)

Remove crusts from bread; cut into 2-inch cubes. Melt cheese and butter in double boiler. Cool slightly. Fold in egg whites. Dip cubes into this mixture to cover. Place on ungreased cookie sheet and refrigerate overnight. Bake at 350 degrees for 10 minutes. Serve hot. Two loaves require 3 recipes of cheese mixture. Makes 110 cubes.

BILL'S HOT CRAB DIP FOR A CROWD

3 bunches green onions,
  finely chopped (tops and
  bottoms)
4 tablespoons margarine
2 pounds crab meat, flaked
  and cartilage removed
5 pounds cream cheese

juice of 8 fresh lemons
cayenne pepper to taste
1 teaspoon Tabasco (or more
  to taste)
1 tablespoon Worcestershire
  sauce

Cook onions in margarine until translucent. Heat cheese in top of double boiler and add onions, crab meat, lemon juice, pepper, Tabasco and Worcestershire. Stir to mix and heat thoroughly. Transfer to chafing dish and serve with small toasts or tortilla chips.

SHOEPEG CORN DIP OR SALSA

1 can shoepeg corn, drained
1 tomato, peeled and chopped
  (drain on paper towel)
1 bell pepper, chopped finely

1 jalapeño, seeds removed
  and chopped finely
  (optional)
1 tablespoon mayonnaise
dash of salt

Mix together; refrigerate. Good on crackers (or as salad).

CRAB MEAT CANAPÉ

1 6½-ounce can crab meat, drained and cartilage removed
¼ cup lemon juice
2 3-ounce packages cream cheese
¼ cup heavy cream
¼ cup mayonnaise
1 teaspoon prepared horseradish
1 teaspoon minced onion
½ clove garlic, crushed
pinch of salt
⅛ teaspoon Worcestershire sauce
4 drops Tabasco sauce

Marinate crab meat in lemon juice for one hour. Whip cream cheese and heavy cream until smooth. Beat in mayonnaise and horseradish. Add onion, chives, garlic and salt. Blend well. Fold drained crab meat into sauce. Add Worcestershire sauce and Tabasco sauce. Spread on melba rounds and run under broiler until bubbly or chill and serve as dip with crackers or party rye. Yields 2 cups.

CHRISTMAS CROSTINI

1 French baguette
1 8-ounce package cream cheese, softened
½ cup mayonnaise
1 0.7-ounce package Italian salad dressing mix
½ cup (2 ounces) shredded Swiss cheese
Garnishes: quartered cucumber slices, finely chopped sweet red pepper

Slice baguette into 36 (¼ to ½ inch) slices; place, cut side down, on an aluminum foil-lined baking sheet. Bake at 400 degrees for 5 minutes or until lightly browned. Combine cream cheese and next 3 ingredients; spread mixture evenly on bread slices. Bake at 400 degrees for 5 minutes or until cheese melts. Garnish, if desired, and serve immediately. Yields 3 dozen.

CHEESE STRAWS

1 cup sifted all purpose flour
½ teaspoon baking powder
1 cup grated Cheddar cheese
½ cup butter (or margarine)
¼ teaspoon cayenne
(optional)
3 tablespoons water

Preheat oven to 450 degrees. Sift flour and baking powder into bowl. Cut in cheese and butter. Add cayenne. Add water and mix well. Roll and cut into strips. Place on ungreased cookie sheet and cook 8 to 10 minutes until lightly browned. Yields 2 dozen.

STUFFED DATES

8 large dates, pitted and split
    in half
¼ cup or 2 ounces fromage
    blanc (soft goat cheese)
1 tablespoon sugar
¼ teaspoon vanilla
¼ teaspoon finely shredded
    orange peel
1 tablespoon finely chopped
    walnuts, toasted
fresh mint for garnish

Mix together the cheese, sugar, vanilla and orange peel. Stuff 16 date halves with mixture. Sprinkle a pinch of nuts on each. Serve on fresh mint. Yields 16 servings.

DEDE'S SPICY CREAM CHEESE TOPPER

1 16-ounce jar apricot
    preserves
1 16-ounce jar pineapple
    preserves
1 12-ounce jar apple jelly
1 1-ounce can dry mustard
1 6-ounce bottle prepared
    horseradish (or to taste)

Mix all ingredients. Serve over cream cheese with crackers. Yields 6 cups and can be stored in covered jars for up to two months in refrigerator. You either love this or think it's much too hot!

CRAB TRIANGLES

8 tablespoons margarine, softened
1 5-ounce jar sharp processed cheese spread (Old English)
1½ teaspoons mayonnaise

8 ounces fresh lump crab meat (or canned), cartilage removed
½ teaspoon garlic powder
½ teaspoon salt
6 English muffins, split

Combine margarine, cheese and mayonnaise. Add remaining ingredients to make a spread. Place heaping tablespoonfuls on each muffin half and spread. Place on cookie sheet and freeze for 1 hour. Remove and cut into quarters. Bag and return to freezer. Bake at 350 degrees for 15-20 minutes when ready to use. Makes 48.

CORN CUPS

6 tablespoons butter (¾ stick) at room temperature
3 ounces cream cheese at room temperature

1 cup flour
½ cup cornmeal
pinch of salt

Preheat oven to 350 degrees. Cream together butter and cream cheese. Combine flour, cornmeal and salt. Add a little at a time to butter mixture until well mixed. Knead lightly. Divide dough into 1-inch balls and press into small muffin tins, using thumb to mold. Make as even as possible and up to top of tins. Bake 20 minutes. Fill with chili, sautéed peppers and chicken, or whatever your heart's delight.

ROASTED GARLIC

4 garlic clusters
4 tablespoons olive oil

4 teaspoons crushed
   rosemary (or other
   herbs)
⅓ cup water

Preheat oven to 350 degrees. Cut tops off garlic clusters. Remove the papery outer skin from the garlic, leaving the cluster intact. Place in a garlic cooker or Pyrex dish. Sprinkle olive oil evenly over garlic, then cover with rosemary. Roast covered loosely with foil about 1 hour until garlic is soft. Serve with toast points and goat cheese as a spread (goat cheese served on an English ivy leaf is very pretty). Serves 4 as an appetizer or more if used as a spread.

Garlic really is a vegetable. It's a member of the lily family, which includes onions, shallots, leeks, and scallions — all vegetables as well. All these are strongly flavored and most often used as seasonings, but they all are delicious when cooked alone. Noonday, Texas, has a festival celebrating the delicious, sweet onions grown on its nearby farms.

GREEN CHILIE CHEESE SQUARES

2 4-ounce cans chopped
   green chilies

10 ounces sharp Cheddar
   cheese, grated
4 eggs, beaten

Preheat oven to 325 degrees. Thoroughly drain cans of chilies. Put in strainer and press out all of juice. Place drained chilies in a 10-inch square greased baking dish. Grate cheese and sprinkle over mixture. Pour beaten eggs over cheese and bake 35 minutes. Cut in squares and serve hot. Serves 6.

GREEN PEPPER SPICED HAM MOLD FOR A CROWD

2 tablespoons green
    peppercorns
8 to 10 slivers of garlic
2 teaspoons cinnamon
6 ounces unsalted butter,
    softened

salt to taste
12 cups ground smoked ham
    (about 6 pounds)
8 tablespoons Dijon mustard
12 tablespoons mayonnaise
    (may need more)

Crush green peppercorns well with garlic and cinnamon in mortar and pestle or use small food processor. Cream in butter and salt to taste. Mix with ham. Add mustard and just enough mayonnaise to bind. Pack into two 6 cup ring molds. Chill until firm. Fill center with tiny spiced onions. Serve with miniature hot biscuits, baguettes or crackers. Serves 50.

GINGER DIP

1 cup mayonnaise
1 cup sour cream
¼ cup chopped green onions
¼ cup minced parsley
¼ cup chopped water
    chestnuts

2 tablespoons minced candied
    ginger, finely chopped
2 cloves garlic, minced, or ½
    teaspoon garlic powder
1 tablespoon soy sauce

Combine all ingredients. Serve with crudités. Yields 2 cups.

HUMUS

2 cups chick peas
1 teaspoon salt
3 cloves garlic, very finely
    chopped

¼ to ½ cup vegetable oil
¼ cup lemon juice

Put all ingredients in a blender. Puree to desired consistency. Serve on pita chips. Yields 1½ cups.

17

JALAPEÑO PIE

4 jalapeños, seeded
⅓ cup chopped water
  chestnuts

10 ounces Cheddar cheese,
  grated
¼ teaspoon salt
4 eggs, beaten

Preheat oven to 300 degrees. Slice peppers into strips. Line a 9-inch Pyrex pie plate with strips in a spoke-wheel pattern. Sprinkle water chestnuts over this and cover with cheese. Gently press cheese into first two layers. Sprinkle with salt. Swirl eggs over surface and bake 25 to 30 minutes. Turn heat off and open door. After 10 minutes remove and cut in wedges to serve. Serves 6.

MACADAMIA NUT STUFFED CELERY

1 8-ounce package cream
  cheese, softened
8 tablespoons or ½ cup real
  butter, softened
1 tablespoon minced green
  onions

3½ ounces macadamia nuts,
  very finely chopped
1 teaspoon finely grated
  orange rind
celery hearts, cut into desired
  lengths

Beat cream cheese and butter until smooth. Blend well with onion, ½ cup nuts and orange rind. Trim inner ribs of celery stalks into short lengths. Stuff with cream cheese mixture. Press remaining nuts on top. May also be formed into a cheese ball. Makes one 3-inch ball or stuffing for two bunches celery hearts.

MUSHROOMS STUFFED WITH WALNUTS AND CHEESE

12 medium sized fresh
   mushroom caps
1 tablespoon olive oil
1 tablespoon sweet butter
½ cup finely chopped yellow
   onion
2 tablespoons coarsely
   chopped toasted walnuts
1 garlic clove, chopped

5 ounces frozen chopped
   spinach (thoroughly
   defrosted and squeezed
   dry)
2 ounces feta cheese
2 tablespoons fresh dill, or 1
   tablespoon dried dill
salt and pepper to taste

Preheat oven to 400 degrees. Remove mushroom stems and save for another use. Brush caps with a mushroom brush or wipe with a damp cloth. Heat olive oil and butter in skillet. Add onion and cook until tender (about 10 minutes). Add walnuts and garlic to onion and cook for another minute. Add spinach and cook for another 5 minutes. Remove from heat and cool slightly. Stir in cheese, dill, salt and pepper. Stuff mushroom caps, place on a baking sheet and bake 8-10 minutes. Serves 6.

THE BEST ONION DIP

2 large onions (Noonday or
   other sweet onions)
1 tablespoon unsalted butter
1 tablespoon peanut or
   sesame oil
½ cup sour cream

½ cup mayonnaise
¼ teaspoon salt
½ teaspoon cayenne pepper
1 teaspoon red pepper flakes
⅛ teaspoon Tabasco sauce

Finely chop onions and sauté in butter and oil until golden brown, about 20 minutes. Cool and add remaining ingredients. Mix well and chill at least 1 hour. Serve with crackers.

PITA BREAD CRISPS

1 package pita bread pockets
½ cup unsalted butter, melted
garlic salt to taste
lemon pepper seasoning to
    taste
basil or dill to taste
freshly grated Parmesan
    cheese

Preheat oven to 275 or 300 degrees. Cut pita bread into pie-shaped wedges and separate. Brush melted butter over wedges and sprinkle with garlic salt, lemon pepper, basil, dill and cheese, or your own favorite combination of seasonings. Bake until crisp and light, about 15 to 20 minutes. Watch carefully to avoid burning. Cool. Serve with cocktails, soups, salads and dips. Freezes well.

PEPPER JELLY TURNOVERS

1 5-ounce jar Old English
    cheese
½ cup butter
1 cup flour
2 tablespoons water
1 4-ounce jar hot pepper jelly
    or 1 4-ounce jar orange
    marmalade

Cut cheese and butter into flour. Quickly stir in water and shape into a ball. Refrigerate overnight. Roll out dough very thin and cut with a biscuit cutter into 2-inch circles. Place ½ teaspoon of pepper jelly in center of each circle. Fold over and crimp edges with a fork. Bake at 375 degrees for 10 minutes. Turnovers may be frozen before or after baking. Reheat before serving. Turnovers may be filled with orange marmalade and dusted with powdered sugar for serving with morning coffee. Yields 2 dozen.

STUFFED PEPPER STRIPS

6 ounces blue cheese
1 8-ounce package softened
　cream cheese
¼ cup fresh chopped chives
　(1 tablespoon dried)
¼ cup chopped parsley

1 large pimento, chopped (or
　one small jar, drained)
salt and pepper to taste
2 tablespoons soft butter
3 green peppers

Combine blue cheese, cream cheese, chives, parsley, pimento, salt, pepper and butter. Mix until smooth. Cut peppers into quarters lengthwise. Remove seeds. Fill strips with cheese mixture and chill until firm. Cut in half lengthwise again and serve on relish tray or fresh vegetable platter. Can also spread half the mixture on sliced squash and half on peppers for variety. Serves 10.

DEVILED SHRIMP

4 pounds raw shrimp in shell
2 lemons, thinly sliced
2 red onions, thinly sliced
1 cup pitted ripe olives
4 tablespoons chopped
　pimento
1 cup freshly squeezed lemon
　juice

½ cup salad oil
2 tablespoons wine vinegar
2 cloves garlic, crushed
1 bay leaf, broken in half
2 tablespoons dry mustard
½ teaspoon cayenne pepper
freshly ground pepper
2 teaspoons salt

Shell and devein raw shrimp. Bring water to boil and add shrimp. Cook for 3 minutes. Drain at once. Combine with lemon and onion slices, olives and pimento in a bowl. Combine lemon juice, oil, vinegar and seasonings in another bowl. Pour over shrimp mixture and toss. Cover and refrigerate overnight, stirring once or twice. To serve, spoon from bowl onto small plates or provide picks for spearing. Serves 10-12.

SHRIMP TOAST

1 3-ounce package cream
cheese, room
temperature

1 stick butter, room
temperature
1 small can shrimp, drained
1 loaf thin sliced white bread

Preheat oven to 350 degrees. Combine cream cheese and butter well; mix in shrimp. Trim crust from thin white bread and spread bread generously with mixture (can be frozen at this point). When ready to serve, cut in quarters and bake for 20 minutes. Serves 10.

SHRIMP FILLED TARTS

1 can baby shrimp (or 15
fresh, cooked and
chopped)
¾ pound grated sharp
Cheddar cheese

1 cup mayonnaise
¼ cup grated onion
dash Worcestershire sauce
1 small jar stuffed green
olives, chopped

Combine all ingredients. Fill tart shells (also can be used to fill cream puff shells). Can be used as a dip. Yields 4-5 dozen tiny tart shells.

HAZEL'S SHRIMP DIP

30 to 40 medium shrimp
1 8-ounce package cream
cheese, softened
½ cup good quality
mayonnaise
2 tablespoons ketchup

1 tablespoon Worcestershire
sauce
1 tablespoon Tabasco sauce
1 teaspoon garlic powder
2 tablespoons onion, minced
salt and pepper to taste

Cook shrimp in boiling water for 5 minutes. Drain well. Clean and devein shrimp and chop finely. Let cool. Blend cream cheese and mayonnaise thoroughly. Add shrimp and remaining ingredients. Mix well. Serve cold with chips or crackers. Serves 40.

1-2-3 SPINACH DIP

1 10-ounce package frozen
   chopped spinach,
   defrosted
2 cups mayonnaise

3 green onions, cut into
   1-inch pieces
garlic salt and pepper to taste

Squeeze spinach until almost dry. Place green onions and mayonnaise in processor bowl. Process with metal blade. Add spinach and process until blended. Season to taste with garlic salt and pepper. Chill. Serve with tortilla chips. Yields 3 cups.

MUSHROOM PÂTÉ

6 slices bacon
1 medium yellow onion,
   chopped
1 clove garlic, minced
1 cup fresh mushrooms,
   chopped
2 tablespoons flour

1 teaspoon Worcestershire
   sauce
½ teaspoon salt, optional
¼ teaspoon pepper
8 ounces sour cream
1 teaspoon soy sauce

Cook bacon until crisp, drain and reserve 2 tablespoons of drippings. Crumble bacon and set aside. Sauté onion and garlic in reserved bacon drippings. Add mushrooms and cook until tender and moisture has evaporated. Stir in flour, Worcestershire sauce, salt, pepper and cream cheese. Blend well. Stir in sour cream and soy sauce. Heat without boiling. Sprinkle top with crumbled bacon. Serve warm with crackers. Yields 2½ cups.

ROSEMARY WALNUTS

6 tablespoons butter
1 tablespoon ground
  rosemary

1 teaspoon salt
½ teaspoon cayenne pepper
4 cups walnut halves

Preheat oven to 300 degrees. Melt butter in a large skillet. Add remaining ingredients and sauté walnuts 5 minutes over medium heat. Stir constantly as walnuts will burn. Pour walnuts into an oven roasting pan. Bake 20 minutes stirring every 5 minutes. Can be made ahead of time and stored in refrigerator. Yields 4 cups.

Tyler's Azalea and Spring Flower Trail is successful because local homeowners work year round to increase their azalea and bulb plantings, and spend countless hours making sure their yards are beautiful for the eyes of visitors. Young ladies in antebellum costumes welcome visitors along the trail.

AZALEA PINK MARGARITA

1 cup chopped frozen
  strawberries
1 small peeled banana
  (optional)
4½ ounces tequila

1½ ounces triple sec
2½ tablespoons fresh lemon
  juice
1 cup cracked ice

Puree all ingredients in a blender until smooth, but still frozen. Serves 2.

AZALEA BREEZE

3 ounces vodka (optional)
⅔ cup pineapple juice

⅔ cup cranberry juice
2 slices lime

In a small pitcher, stir together vodka, pineapple juice and cranberry juice. Pour into 2 glasses filled with ice. Garnish with lime. Serves 2.

WONDERFUL EGGNOG

1 pint heavy cream
1¼ cups sugar, divided use
6 eggs, separated
¾ cup bourbon
⅓ cup light rum
1 quart milk
nutmeg to taste

Whip cream until stiff, adding ¼ cup sugar. Separate eggs. Whip egg whites very stiff, adding ½ cup sugar. Whip egg yolks until creamy, adding ½ cup sugar. Continue beating until sugar is dissolved. Add the whiskey and rum to the yolk mixture and mix well. Stir in the milk. Fold in egg whites, thoroughly, then the whipped cream. This eggnog can be made up a day in advance and refrigerated. Serve in punch cups and sprinkle with nutmeg.

PEACH SLUSH

½ overripe peach
1 heaping teaspoon sugar
3 ounces whiskey
1 cup crushed ice

Mash the peach and sugar together; add whiskey. Pour over crushed ice in blender and mix until smooth. Serves 1.

COFFEE ICE CREAM PUNCH

1 quart vanilla ice cream
3 cups milk
¼ cup sugar
1 teaspoon vanilla
¾ teaspoon ground nutmeg
6 cups freshly brewed coffee, cooled
coffee ice cubes
whipped cream

Spoon ice cream by tablespoons into a large punch bowl. Add milk, sugar, vanilla and nutmeg; stir just until combined. Stir in cooled coffee and coffee ice cubes. Ladle into cups and garnish with whipped cream. Coffee Ice Cubes: Pour 2 cups cooled strong coffee into ice cube tray. Freeze. Serves 24 cups.

BLOODY MARY

1½ ounces vodka
3 ounces tomato juice
½ ounce lemon juice
½ teaspoon Worcestershire
  sauce

pinch of salt and pepper
seasoned salt to taste
¼ teaspoon sugar
3 drops Tabasco sauce

Combine all ingredients and serve over ice. Garnish with celery stick or dill pickle. Serves 1.

SUMMER SAVORY

4 large handfuls mint
juice of 6 lemons
grated peel and juice of 2
  oranges

2 cups sugar
2½ cups water

Wash mint. Boil sugar and water together for 10 minutes. Pour hot syrup over juices and mint. Let steep, covered, for several hours. Strain in jars and store in refrigerator. Use in mixed drinks, iced tea, or freeze for slush.

TOMATO WOW

1 46-ounce can tomato juice
½ of 6-ounce can orange
  juice concentrate
juice of 2 lemons

juice of 1 lime
1 tablespoon Worcestershire
  sauce
2 teaspoons salt

Blend and chill. Serve in frosted glasses.

RUBY WATERMELON PUNCH

½ cup sugar
½ cup water
¾ cup frozen pink lemonade,
  thawed

1½ cups cranberry juice
  cocktail
1 28-ounce bottle ginger ale,
  chilled
½ large watermelon

Boil sugar and water for 5 minutes. Blend in lemonade and cranberry juice and chill mixture in freezer until icy. Make 2 cups melon balls from watermelon. Remove most meat from watermelon to create a serving bowl. Chill balls and rind thoroughly. At serving time, blend cranberry juice mixture, ginger ale, and melon balls and serve in chilled rind bowl. Yields 3 quarts.

MOCK CHAMPAGNE PUNCH

1 6-ounce can frozen
lemonade concentrate
1 6-ounce can frozen
pineapple juice
concentrate
2 cups cold water
2 7-ounce bottles ginger ale,
chilled

2 7-ounce bottles sparkling
water
1 large bottle sparkling grape
juice
ice ring of cubes containing
mint leaves and
strawberries

Pour concentrates and water into a punch bowl and mix. Float ice ring on top. Carefully pour ginger ale, sparkling water and grape juice down inside of bowl. Yields 2 quarts.

MANGO DAIQUIRI

1 cup chopped peeled mango
3 ounces dark rum
1 tablespoon sugar
(preferably superfine)

2 teaspoons fresh lime juice
2 cups cracked ice

Blend all ingredients in blender until smooth but still frozen. Serves 1.

CITRUS TEA PUNCH

1½ cups water
1 tea bag, family size
1½ cups orange juice
1½ cups pineapple juice
½ cup lemon juice

1 cup sugar
3 cups chilled ginger ale
orange or lemon slices
(optional)

Bring water to a boil in a large saucepan; add tea bag. Remove from heat, cover and let stand 5 minutes. Remove tea bag. Add fruit juices and sugar, stirring until sugar dissolves. Chill. Stir in ginger ale just before serving. Add slices of fruit, if desired. Yields 2 quarts.

GRAPEFRUIT SURPRISE

2 6-ounce cans frozen
   grapefruit juice
   concentrate
6 6-ounce cans water
1½ cups brandy

½ cup maraschino cherry
   syrup
cracked ice
8 stemmed maraschino
   cherries

Place first 4 ingredients in a blender. Blend until smooth. Place in freezer until needed. Pour over cracked ice in wine glasses and garnish with cherry.

WASSAIL BOWL PUNCH

1 quart tea
1 quart cranberry juice
   cocktail
1 quart apple juice
3 cinnamon sticks

12 whole cloves
2 cups orange juice
1 6-ounce can frozen
   lemonade, undiluted

Mix all ingredients over low heat. Cool slightly and pour into punch bowl. Serve warm.

BANANA SLUSH PUNCH

6 cups water
4 cups sugar
1 48-ounce can pineapple
   juice
1 48-ounce can orange juice

juice of 4 lemons
5 bananas (put through
   blender)
2-3 liter bottles of ginger ale

Heat water and sugar until dissolved. Cool. Mix with other ingredients. Freeze in rings until needed. Allow to thaw 2 or 3 hours before using. Place in punch bowl and add 2 bottles of ginger ale. Stir until "slushy". Serves 20-30.

Breads

Gilmer East Texas Yamboree

The Yamboree, a tribute to the region's mouth-watering yam, is an extravaganza that has been held during the third weekend of October since 1935. When bountiful yam crops are newly harvested, the celebration begins.

The Yamboree features a wide array of activities and attractions, including hobby and craft shows, yam pie judging, art exhibits, livestock shows and area bands.

The Yamboree Ball and Carnival, the Tour de Yam Bicycle Ride, Tater Trot 5K and the Yamboree Parade are an exciting part of the festival. Crowning the event is the presentation of the Yamboree Queen!

BUTTERMILK BISCUITS

3 cups sifted flour
1 teaspoon salt
3½ teaspoons baking powder

½ cup plus 2 tablespoons butter (at room temperature)
1¼ cups buttermilk, divided use

Preheat oven to 425 degrees. Sift dry ingredients together and cut in butter. Gradually add 1 cup buttermilk. Knead lightly by hand to make soft dough (to ensure flaky biscuits, do not over-mix or over-handle). Turn dough onto lightly floured surface, and roll out to ¾-inch thickness. Cut into 2-inch biscuit rounds. Arrange biscuits 1 inch apart on ungreased baking sheet. For softer biscuits, set rounds closer together. Brush tops with remaining ¼ cup buttermilk. Bake 12 - 15 minutes.

BREAKFAST CAKE

½ cup soft butter
¾ cup sugar
1 egg
2 cups flour

2 teaspoons baking powder
½ teaspoon salt
½ cup milk
2 cups blueberries

Topping:
½ teaspoon cinnamon
½ cup brown sugar, packed
¼ cup flour

¼ cup butter, cut in small pieces

Preheat oven to 375 degrees. Cream together butter and sugar. Add egg. Sift flour, baking powder and salt together. Add sifted ingredients alternately with milk to creamed mixture. Fold in blueberries (batter should be thick). Spread in buttered 9 x 13-inch baking dish. Mix together topping ingredients. Sprinkle batter with topping and bake for 30 to 35 minutes.

DANISH PUFF

1 cup water
½ cup margarine
1 teaspoon almond extract

1 cup flour
3 eggs

Glaze:
1½ cups powdered sugar
2 tablespoons margarine

1½ teaspoons vanilla
2 tablespoons warm water

Preheat oven to 350 degrees. To make the puff: In a medium saucepan boil water and margarine. Remove from heat. Quickly stir in almond extract and flour. Stir vigorously over low heat until mixture forms a ball (about 1 minute). Remove from heat. Beat in eggs, all at once, until smooth and glossy. Spread mixture on buttered cookie sheet and bake for 1 hour. Cool. Combine ingredients for glaze, and spread on cooled puffs. Sprinkle with finely chopped nuts. Cut into parallelograms. Yields 3 dozen.

KOLACHES

2 packages dry yeast
¼ cup lukewarm water
1 teaspoon sugar
¾ cup margarine or butter
¾ cup sugar
2 egg yolks
2 teaspoons salt

6 cups flour
2 cups milk
1 cup sugar
½ cup flour
1 teaspoon cinnamon
2 tablespoons margarine or
   butter, melted

Dissolve yeast in ¼ cup **WARM** water and add 1 teaspoon sugar. Cream ¾ cup sugar and ¾ cup butter in large bowl. Add egg yolks and salt. Mix well. Add yeast and ½ cup flour. Mix slowly. Add milk and slowly add remaining flour, mixing well. Cover and let rise in a warm place until double in bulk; about 1 hour. Roll dough into balls (about a tablespoonful each) and place on buttered cookie sheet about an inch apart. Let rise until light. Make an indentation in center of each piece and fill with crumb topping. Crumb Topping: Mix 1 cup sugar, ½ cup flour, 1 teaspoon cinnamon and 2 tablespoons melted butter, until it resembles a coarse meal. Sprinkle topping on each kolache and bake at 425 degrees for 15 minutes. Butter kolaches upon removal from oven, and cool on wire rack.

BEER BREAD

3 cups self-rising flour
1 12-ounce can beer (room
temperature)

3 tablespoons sugar
butter for top

Preheat oven to 350 degrees. Sift flour and sugar six times. Add beer and mix until moistened. Pour into oiled loaf pan. Bake 45 minutes at 350 degrees. Remove from oven and butter the top. Bake 15 more minutes. Yields 1 loaf.

BROWN BREAD

3 cups raisins
3 teaspoons baking soda
2 tablespoons margarine
1 teaspoon salt
2 cups boiling water
1 teaspoon vanilla

2 eggs
2 cups sugar
4 cups flour
3 tablespoons molasses
1 cup walnuts

Preheat oven to 350 degrees. Place raisins, soda, margarine and salt into a large bowl. Pour in boiling water. Let stand 2 hours or overnight. Add vanilla, eggs, sugar, flour, molasses and walnuts. Stir together. Butter a 1-pound coffee can and fill ¾ full with batter. Place can on a baking sheet and bake for 1 hour. Remove and empty contents onto wire rack to cool. Yields 2 loaves.

WELSH SCONES

4 tablespoons butter (½ stick)
1¾ cups flour
¼ teaspoon salt
5½ tablespoons sugar

1 teaspoon soda
2 teaspoons cream of tartar
2 eggs
⅓ cup milk

Preheat oven to 450 degrees. Cut butter into flour and salt, mixing until like coarse cornmeal. Add sugar, baking soda, and cream of tartar. Mix well. Beat eggs with milk and add to flour to create a spongy mixture. Pat dough onto a well-floured surface to ½ inch thickness. Cut with a biscuit cutter. Place on greased cookie sheet to rest 10 minutes. Bake in preheated oven for 8 minutes. Serve with butter, cream, or jam. Yields 12 scones.

CRANBERRY BREAD

1¾ cups flour
1 cup sugar
1½ teaspoons baking powder
1 teaspoon salt
½ teaspoon baking soda
⅓ cup butter
1 egg

1 teaspoon grated orange
    rind
¾ cup orange juice
½ cup walnuts
2 cups raw cranberries,
    halved

Preheat oven to 350 degrees. In large bowl blend dry ingredients. Blend in margarine by cutting into dry ingredients until consistency is that of coarse meal. Beat egg, orange juice and rind. Add to dry ingredients, along with nuts and cranberries. Bake at 350 degrees for 45 minutes in a buttered loaf pan. Turn out on wire rack to cool. Yields 1 loaf.

BLUEBERRY BREAD WITH ZEST

2 cups blueberries, fresh or
    frozen (reserve ½ cup)
½ cup butter or margarine
2 large eggs or egg substitute
1 cup sugar
½ teaspoon salt
2 teaspoons baking powder
2¼ cups flour, measured
    before sifting

½ cup milk
1½ teaspoons lemon extract
2 teaspoons lemon rind,
    grated
2 tablespoons wheat germ
1 tablespoon cinnamon sugar
    for top of bread

Preheat oven to 350 degrees. Rinse fresh or frozen berries just before using. Drain on paper towel. DO NOT THAW FROZEN BERRIES AS THEY STAY JUICIER WHEN USED FROZEN. Allow butter to soften in bowl. Add eggs and sugar and beat well. In a separate bowl, combine salt, baking powder, flour and wheat germ. Add to butter, egg and sugar mixture and then stir in milk. Beat lightly. Fold blueberries into batter gently. Spoon batter into a well-oiled, floured pan. Sprinkle reserved berries on top and press in. Cover batter with cinnamon-sugar mixture. Bake 45 to 50 minutes or until a knife when inserted comes out clean. DO NOT OVERCOOK, as it will dry the bread. Better to slightly undercook. Yields 1 loaf.

BREAD IN A JAR

⅔ cup shortening
2⅔ cups sugar
4 eggs
⅔ cup water
3⅓ cups flour
½ teaspoon baking powder

2 teaspoons soda
1½ teaspoons salt
1 teaspoon cinnamon
1 teaspoon cloves
2 cups pumpkin

Preheat oven to 325 degrees. Wash and dry 8 pint-size **wide mouth** canning jars. Butter well. Cream shortening and sugar together. Add eggs, one at a time. Add water and then flour, baking powder, soda, salt, cinnamon and cloves. Mix lightly and add 2 cups pumpkin, or 2 cups fruit or vegetable of your choice. Fill jars ½ full. Bake on middle rack of oven for 45 - 55 minutes. **Variations:** Omit pumpkin and add: 2 cups shredded apples, or 2 cups shredded carrots, or 2 cups shredded zucchini or 2 cups mashed banana. Yields 8 jars.

LEMON BREAD

1 cup margarine
2 cups sugar
4 eggs
½ teaspoon salt
½ teaspoon soda

3 cups sifted flour
1 cup buttermilk
grated rind of one lemon
1 cup chopped nuts

Glaze:
juice of 2 lemons

1 cup powdered sugar

Preheat oven to 300 degrees. Cream margarine and sugar. Blend in eggs. Add sifted dry ingredients alternately with buttermilk. Add lemon rind and nuts. Grease two large loaf pans. Line bottom of pans with wax paper. Bake for 40 minutes. Test. If not done, lower oven temperature and cook until done. Mix lemon juice and powdered sugar for glaze. Punch holes in bread with toothpick and pour glaze over bread while still warm. Yields 2 loaves.

PISTACHIO NUT BREAD

1½ cups all purpose flour
½ cup whole wheat flour
1 teaspoon baking powder
½ teaspoon baking soda
½ teaspoon salt
¼ cup chopped pistachio nuts
1 tablespoon brown sugar
¼ teaspoon dried whole
    rosemary

⅛ teaspoon ground saffron
    (optional)
¾ cup low fat buttermilk
2 tablespoons olive oil
1 egg
vegetable cooking spray
1 egg white, beaten

Preheat oven to 375 degrees. Combine first 9 ingredients in large bowl; make a well in center of flour mixture. Combine the next 3 ingredients and stir. Add to well in dry mixture, stirring until dry ingredients are just moistened. Turn dough out onto a floured surface, and knead lightly several times. Shape into a ball. Place ball of dough on a baking sheet coated with cooking spray. Gently cut slits in top of loaf, using a sharp knife. Brush loaf with egg white. Bake at 375 degrees for 25 - 30 minutes, or until golden and loaf sounds hollow when tapped. Remove bread from baking sheet, and let cool 5 minutes on a wire rack. Cut into slices and serve warm. Makes 12 servings.

SHARLOTTE'S CHRISTMAS PUMPKIN BREAD

1½ cups white sugar
1½ cups brown sugar
4 eggs
1 cup salad oil
4 teaspoons cinnamon
2 teaspoons nutmeg
¼ teaspoon ginger

½ teaspoon cloves
½ teaspoon mace
2 teaspoons soda
½ teaspoon salt
2 cups canned pumpkin
⅔ cup water
3½ cups flour

Preheat oven to 350 degrees. Mix first 12 ingredients in a large bowl. Add water and flour alternately. Mix in nuts or raisins if desired. Pour into well-buttered and floured loaf pans. Cook for 50 minutes. Yields 2 large or 5 small loaves, or use coffee cans for an interesting shape.

RAISIN BREAD

⅓ cup oleo, softened
⅔ cup sugar
2 teaspoons grated lemon
    peel
¼ teaspoon cinnamon
2 eggs
3 tablespoons milk
1 teaspoon lemon juice

2 cups flour
1 teaspoon baking powder
1 teaspoon salt
½ teaspoon baking soda
1½ cups peeled, shredded
    apple
1 cup raisins
½ cup chopped walnuts

Preheat oven to 350 degrees. Cream first 4 ingredients. Beat in eggs until light and fluffy. Beat in milk and lemon juice. Stir together dry ingredients, and add to the cream mixture. Stir until moistened. Fold in apple, raisins and nuts. Bake in greased and floured loaf pan, also lining bottom of pan with wax paper, for 50 - 60 minutes or until done. Yields 1 loaf.

TOMATO-CILANTRO BREAD

2 cups flour
1 teaspoon baking soda
1 tablespoon baking powder
1 teaspoon salt
1 teaspoon ground cumin
½ to 1 cup fresh cilantro
    leaves

3 whole green onions, cut
    into 2-inch strips
6 plum tomatoes, seeded and
    quartered
2 tablespoons tomato paste
¾ cup sugar
3 large eggs (or 6 ounces egg
    substitute)

Preheat oven to 350 degrees. Place flour, baking soda, baking powder, salt and cumin in food processor with metal blade, and process for a few seconds. Switch these ingredients to another bowl. Process the cilantro and the onion for a few seconds. Add tomatoes and tomato paste. Process until tomatoes are pureed. Add sugar and process. Scrape down sides of bowl. Add eggs and process until mixture is fluffy. Add dry ingredients. Combine until mixture is just mixed well. Pour mixture into a 9 x 5-inch pan which has been sprayed with vegetable cooking spray. Spread mixture evenly, and bake at 350 degrees for 45 minutes, or until browned. Let bread cool in pan for 10 minutes, then turn onto wire rack to cool. The aroma of this bread while baking is heavenly. Great served with southwestern food, and will be de-voured quickly. Yields 1 loaf.

BREAD MACHINE COTTAGE CHEESE BREAD

2¼ teaspoons dry powdered yeast
3 cups bread flour (or 1½ cups white and 1½ cups whole wheat)
½ teaspoon lite salt
¼ teaspoon baking soda
2 teaspoons sugar

1 egg (or 2 ounces egg substitute)
1 tablespoon margarine
1 tablespoon applesauce (to cut fat)
1 cup non-fat cottage cheese
¼ cup water

Place ingredients in bread machine according to manufacturer's instructions. Set on white bread setting; medium crust. Enjoy warm and wonderful bread in a few hours. Yields 1½ pound loaf.

BREAD MACHINE DILL BREAD

1⅓ cups non-fat cottage cheese
2½ eggs (or equivalent egg substitute)
2 tablespoons plus 1 teaspoon sugar

2 tablespoons dill weed
1 teaspoon lite salt
⅓ teaspoon baking soda
3½ cups bread flour
2¼ teaspoons yeast

Place ingredients into bread machine according to manufacturer's instructions. Set on white bread setting; medium crust. A great hot bread in a few hours. Yields 1½ pound loaf.

Gilmer's Yamboree celebrates the sweet potato which is often called the near perfect food because of its high nutritional value. It is loaded with Vitamin A and has impressive amounts of potassium and calcium. Local cooks feel that baking is a grand way to enjoy the sweet potato at its best. To bake, scrub and dry potato, pierce with a fork, place on a sheet of aluminum foil, and bake at 400 degrees until soft when pinched — about 45 minutes. Serve with butter, brown sugar or honey, and spices. Microwave baking is also successful. Enjoy!

APPLESAUCE BRAN MUFFINS

1½ cups (100 percent) bran
1½ cups applesauce
1 egg
¼ cup margarine, melted
½ cup packed light brown
   sugar

1½ cups flour
1 tablespoon baking powder
1 teaspoon cinnamon
½ cup seedless raisins
½ cup powdered sugar
1 tablespoon applesauce

Preheat oven to 400 degrees. Mix bran, applesauce, egg, margarine and brown sugar. Let stand 5 minutes. In large bowl blend flour, baking powder and cinnamon; stir in bran mixture just until blended (batter will be lumpy). Stir in raisins. Spoon into 12 oiled or sprayed muffin cups. Bake for 15 to 18 minutes. Glaze: Blend powdered sugar with 1 tablespoon applesauce. Drizzle onto hot muffins. Makes 1 dozen.

BANANA MUFFINS

1 cup sugar
1 cup margarine
1 cup mashed banana
   (2 large)
4½ tablespoons buttermilk
2 eggs, slightly beaten
1½ cups sifted flour

1 teaspoon soda
1 teaspoon cinnamon
1 teaspoon nutmeg
¼ teaspoon salt
1 teaspoon vanilla
1 cup pecans, chopped

Preheat oven to 325 degrees. Cream sugar and margarine. Add bananas, buttermilk and eggs. Mix dry ingredients and fold into banana mixture. Add vanilla. Pour into buttered muffin pans and bake for 30 minutes. Yields 14-16.

BASIC MUFFINS

2 cups sifted flour
4 teaspoons baking powder
½ teaspoon salt
½ to ¾ cup sugar

2 eggs, well beaten
1 cup milk
4 tablespoons butter

Preheat oven to 425 degrees. Mix and sift dry ingredients. Mix egg and milk and stir into dry ingredients. Stir in melted butter. Bake in greased muffin tins, ¾ full, for 20 to 25 minutes. Yields 12 medium or 24 small muffins. **Variations:** Blueberry Muffins: Carefully fold in 1 cup blueberries, fresh or unthawed frozen. Nut Muffins: Add ½ cup toasted nut meats.

PLAN AHEAD MUFFINS

1 15-ounce box bran flakes or
   raisin bran
3 cups sugar
5 cups flour, sifted
3 teaspoons soda

2 teaspoons salt
4 eggs, beaten
1 cup canola oil
1 quart buttermilk

Preheat oven to 400 degrees. Mix dry ingredients in very large bowl. Add eggs, oil, and buttermilk. Mix well. Fill greased muffin cups ⅔ full. Bake 15-20 minutes. Store, covered, in refrigerator and use as needed up to six weeks.

ZUCCHINI NUT MUFFINS

3 eggs
1 cup oil
2 cups sugar
1 tablespoon vanilla
1 teaspoon salt
1 teaspoon baking powder
2 teaspoons soda

2 cups flour
1 tablespoon cinnamon
½ teaspoon nutmeg
1 cup chopped nuts
2 cups zucchini, unpeeled and
   shredded

Preheat oven to 400 degrees. Beat eggs slightly. Add oil, sugar and vanilla. Blend well. Add dry ingredients and nuts. Stir until blended. Stir in zucchini. Spoon batter into muffin cups lined with paper, or buttered well. Bake for 18 to 20 minutes. Yields 18 muffins.

JALAPEÑO CORNBREAD

3 cups cornmeal
3 teaspoons baking powder
3 teaspoons salt
2 tablespoons sugar
2½ cups milk
3 tablespoons cooking oil
1 large onion, chopped
3 eggs, beaten

3 jalapeño peppers, seeded
  and chopped
1½ cups Longhorn cheese,
  grated
2 cups cream style corn
3 to 4 slices bacon, cooked
  crisp and crumbled
1 pimento, chopped

Preheat oven to 400 degrees. Mix all ingredients and bake in three 8 x 8-inch oiled pans for 40 minutes.

PERFECT CORNBREAD

1 cup sifted flour
¼ cup sugar
4 teaspoons baking powder
¾ teaspoons salt

1 cup yellow cornmeal
2 eggs
1 cup milk
¼ cup shortening, melted

Preheat oven to 425 degrees. Sift flour, sugar, baking powder and salt together. Add cornmeal, eggs and milk. Blend well. Stir in shortening. Beat until smooth (1 minute). Pour into a 9 x 9 x 2-inch buttered or sprayed pan, and bake for 20 - 25 minutes.

No smell is more welcoming than that of bread freshly baked from the oven. East Texans everywhere take great pride in baking breads of many types — yeast, sourdough, rolls, or muffins. Probably the regional bread of choice, however, is our cornbread. Young and old cooks take great pride in "their" bread. Families either prefer it with sugar or without — but expect it to always accompany luscious meals of peas, squash, potatoes, and tomatoes when vegetable harvest is at its peak.

SOUR CREAM REFRIGERATOR ROLLS

2 ½-ounce packages dry
   yeast
½ cup WARM water (105 to
   115 degrees)
1 8-ounce carton sour cream,
   scalded (150 degrees)

½ cup sugar
1 teaspoon salt
½ cup margarine, melted
2 eggs, beaten
4 cups all-purpose flour

Preheat oven to 375 degrees. Dissolve yeast in warm water. In a large mixing bowl, mix the scalded sour cream, sugar, salt and margarine. Cool until lukewarm. Stir dissolved yeast into this and mix well. Add beaten eggs. Gradually stir in flour, until the dough is soft. Cover bowl tightly and refrigerate overnight. Divide dough into 4 equal portions. Turn each portion out on a heavily floured surface and knead several times. Roll each into an 8 x 12-inch rectangle. Cut rounds with a 4-inch biscuit cutter. Fold in half and press firmly with palm of hand, making sure that the edges are sealed. Place rolls on buttered cookie sheet and let rise in a warm, draft-free place until doubled in bulk (about 1 hour). Bake for 13 to 16 minutes. Yields 4½ dozen.

APPETIZER CHEESE LOAVES

1 loaf frozen white bread
   dough
melted butter or margarine

1 cup shredded sharp natural
   Cheddar cheese

Preheat oven to 350 degrees. Let well-wrapped dough thaw and warm to room temperature. Knead the shredded cheese into the dough. Divide in half and shape each half into a round ball, flattening slightly. Place rounds of dough on opposite corners of an oiled baking sheet. Cover and let rise in a warm place (80 to 85 degrees) until doubled in size. Bake for 25 to 30 minutes or until loaves are lightly browned and sound hollow when tapped. Immediately remove from baking sheet and place on wire rack to cool. Brush tops with melted butter or margarine while still hot.

CLAY'S CHEESY BREAD

1 long loaf bread (sour dough
   is fine), cut lengthwise
1 pound Swiss cheese, grated
1½ sticks butter
8 green onions, chopped

2 teaspoons lemon juice
2 teaspoons poppy seed
2 teaspoons Dijon mustard
2 teaspoons seasoning salt

Preheat oven to 350 degrees. Melt butter; add all ingredients except cheese. Spread both sides of bread with butter and top with cheese. Bake for 20 minutes. Do not bake longer, as the cheese will become chewy. Slice across. This makes a simple meal into something special.

JOHN NELSON'S ROLLS

1 package active dry yeast
½ cup warm water
½ teaspoon sugar
½ cup shortening
½ cup sugar

1 tablespoon salt
1 egg
2 cups very warm water
6 cups flour

Preheat oven to 375 degrees. Dissolve yeast in 1 cup water. Put in large cup as mixture will foam up. Set aside and add ½ teaspoon sugar. Cream shortening with 1 cup sugar and salt until soft and fluffy (2-3 minutes), then add egg and continue to cream, about 1 minutes. Add 2 cups very warm water. Add yeast mixture. Begin adding flour, 2 cups at a time, mixing well with a spoon. When well mixed, scrape sides of bowl and mound. Cover with a cloth and let rise in a warm area until doubled in size, about 2 hours. Punch down. Store covered in a container with a tight lid. Cut off portions as needed, and roll into inch round balls (or as desired) and let rise about 1 to 2 hours. Bake for 10 to 12 minutes. Will keep about a week. Yields 3 dozen.

Cookies and Candies

Marshall Wonderland of Lights

Marshall becomes a dazzling Wonderland of Lights during the Christmas season. Downtown businesses and neighborhoods are resplendent in brilliant white lights from November 23rd through December 30th.

The spectacular Christmas parade winds through the downtown streets in early December. Also featured is the annual Candlelight Home Tour and special music.

While walking around the town square, visitors can view the fabulous light display and sample the hot apple cider.

DOUBLE CHOCOLATE COOKIE

2 cups flour, sifted
1 teaspoon baking soda
¼ cup granulated sugar
1 4-ounce package instant
    chocolate pudding mix
1 cup butter or margarine

¾ cup light brown sugar,
    packed
1 teaspoon vanilla
2 eggs
1 12-ounce package semi-
    sweet chocolate morsels
1 cup chopped nuts

Preheat oven to 375 degrees. Sift together flour, baking soda and dry pudding mix. In large electric mixer bowl, beat butter, brown sugar, vanilla and eggs until light and fluffy. Gradually add in flour mixture. Stir in chocolate morsels and nuts. Drop dough by heaping teaspoonfuls onto lightly buttered baking sheets. Bake about 10 minutes.

SOFT GINGER COOKIES

1 cup shortening
1 cup brown sugar
½ to ¾ cup molasses
2 eggs
1 cup sour cream
2 teaspoons baking soda

3 cups flour
2 teaspoons ground ginger
2 teaspoons cinnamon
1 teaspoon ground cloves
1 teaspoon ground nutmeg

Frosting:
¾ cup powdered sugar
½ teaspoon lemon extract

half and half

Preheat oven to 375 degrees. Cream shortening and sugar thoroughly. Add molasses and eggs. Mix well. Add baking soda and sour cream; blend well. Beat for 2 minutes. Add flour and seasonings. Mix well. Drop by heaping teaspoonfuls onto lightly buttered cookie sheet. Bake 10 - 12 minutes. Cool and frost. **Frosting:** Mix together powdered sugar and lemon extract. Add half and half until consistency is right to trickle frosting on cookies. Frost cookies and serve.

CHOCOLATE TRUFFLES

1 8-ounce package semi-
　sweet chocolate morsels
4 ounces cream cheese,
　softened
3½ cups (8 ounces) non-
　dairy whipped topping,
　thawed

1½ teaspoons vanilla,
　or 1 tablespoon almond,
　coffee or orange liqueur,
　or 1 tablespoon rum
　(or more to taste)
finely chopped nuts, coconut
　or semi-sweet chocolate,
　grated

Heat chocolate morsels in a large bowl in microwave on high 2 minutes. Stir until completely melted (or heat in heavy saucepan over very low heat). Beat in cream cheese and vanilla (or other flavoring); cool to room temperature. Gently stir ⅓ of whipped topping into chocolate mixture, then stir remaining ⅔ in gently. Refrigerate 1 hour. Shape quickly into 1-inch balls. Roll in nuts, coconut or grated chocolate. Store, covered, in refrigerator. Enjoy! Walk, or jog, 2 miles every day for three weeks to remove excess calories. Yields 3 dozen.

ALMOND RASPBERRY TASSIES

½ cup butter or margarine,
　softened

3 ounces cream cheese
1 cup flour

Filling:
¼ cup raspberry preserves
½ cup sugar
½ cup (2 ounces) almond
　paste

2 egg yolks
3 tablespoons flour
2 tablespoons milk
1 tablespoon orange juice

Preheat oven to 400 degrees. Blend softened butter and cream cheese. Stir in flour. Cover and chill. Divide dough into 24 balls. Press into sides and bottom of small muffin tins. For filling, put ½ teaspoon raspberry preserves into each unbaked shell. Use fork to combine sugar and almond paste. Add egg yolks one at a time, and mix well as each yolk is added. Blend in other ingredients. Spoon into shells. Bake for 15 minutes. Cool before removing from pan. Yields 2 dozen.

ALMOND COOKIE DOUGH

½ pound unsalted butter, at
   room temperature
½ cup powdered sugar
½ teaspoon vanilla extract
½ teaspoon almond extract

2 cups all-purpose flour
¼ teaspoon salt
½ cup finely chopped
   almonds

In mixing bowl with electric mixer, beat butter and sugar until light and fluffy. Add vanilla and almond extract, beating well. Mix in flour, salt and almonds. When well blended, divide dough into thirds. Wrap in plastic wrap and refrigerate until chilled. May be refrigerated up to 5 days. May be frozen. This is a sweet and rich dough that will make Jam Logs and Thumbprints, Candy-Decorated Almond Cookies, and English Currant Tarts, all from the same batter. The added almonds give it an extra crunch. You will be using one-third of the dough for each type of cookie, or you can use it all for any one type of cookie. When ready to use, allow to come to room temperature. Form into cookie of your choice and bake at 325 degrees for 20 minutes or until pale golden.

OATMEAL REFRIGERATOR COOKIES

¾ cup plus 2 tablespoons
   cake flour, sifted
½ teaspoon baking soda
½ teaspoon salt
½ cup soft shortening
½ cup sugar
½ cup brown sugar, packed

1 egg
1½ teaspoons finely grated
   lemon rind
1½ tablespoons molasses
½ teaspoon vanilla
1½ cups uncooked rolled oats
   (quick cooking)

Preheat oven to 400 degrees. Sift together flour, soda and salt. Thoroughly mix shortening with sugars. Add egg, lemon rind, molasses and vanilla. Add flour mixture to egg mixture, then add oats, a few at a time. Press and mold into 2 rolls, 2 inches in diameter. Wrap and refrigerate several hours, or may be frozen until ready to bake. Slice dough ⅛-inch thick and place on unbuttered cookie sheet. Bake 8 to 10 minutes, or until light brown. Yields 4 dozen.

DUTCH REFRIGERATOR COOKIES

1 cup shortening
½ cup white sugar
½ cup brown sugar
1 egg
2¼ cups flour, sifted
½ teaspoon soda

½ teaspoon salt
2 teaspoons cinnamon
¼ teaspoon nutmeg
¼ teaspoon cloves
½ cup nuts, chopped

Preheat oven to 375 degrees. Cream sugars and shortening. Add egg and beat well. Add sifted dry ingredients and nuts. Shape into two rolls and chill. Slice thinly and bake for 10 - 12 minutes. Yields 5-6 dozen.

ORANGE PECAN COOKIES

1 cup margarine
½ cup brown sugar
½ cup white sugar
1 egg
1 teaspoon grated orange
    rind

1 teaspoon orange juice
2¾ cups flour
¼ teaspoon soda
¼ teaspoon salt
½ cup pecans, chopped

Preheat oven to 350 degrees. Cream shortening and sugars. Add egg and blend. Add orange rind and juice; blend. Sift dry ingredients, add and blend. Form into 2 rolls on foil. Enclose each roll in wrap. Chill or freeze overnight. Slice and bake for 10 - 12 minutes, for crisp and thin cookies. Yields 5-6 dozen.

CINNAMON STICKS

1 cup butter
1 cup sugar
1 egg yolk (reserve white)

1 heaping teaspoon
    cinnamon
2 cups flour
1 cup pecans, finely chopped

Preheat oven to 325 degrees. Cream butter and sugar. Add egg yolk and mix well. Add flour sifted with cinnamon and mix well. Pat out as thin as possible on two unbuttered cookie sheets. Spread with egg white. Sprinkle with chopped nuts and bake for 20 - 25 minutes. Cut into 2-inch rectangular sticks while still warm. Yields 4 dozen.

LEMON SHORTBREAD

1½ sticks unsalted butter, at
    room temperature
½ cup powdered sugar
1½ cups unbleached flour
¼ teaspoon salt

½ teaspoon vanilla extract
2 tablespoons finely grated
    lemon zest
2 tablespoons granulated
    sugar

Cream butter and sugar until light. Sift flour and salt into another bowl and add butter mixture. Add vanilla and lemon zest and blend thoroughly. Gather dough into a ball, wrap in wax paper and refrigerate for several hours. Preheat oven to 325 degrees. Remove dough and allow to soften slightly. Press into an 8-inch square cake pan. Sprinkle with sugar and bake 20 minutes or until shortbread starts to brown slightly. Remove, allow to cool, and cut into 4 x 1-inch bars. Yields 16 bars.

CHOCOLATE CHIP MERINGUE COOKIES

2 egg whites
¾ cup sugar
½ teaspoon vanilla

1 6-ounce package semi-
    sweet chocolate chips
1 cup pecans, chopped

Preheat oven to 350 degrees. Beat egg whites until stiff, gradually adding sugar (for a variation, use a pinch of salt with ⅛ teaspoon cream of tartar and ½ teaspoon almond extract instead of sugar). Beat at high speed for 5 minutes. Fold in other ingredients. Drop by scant tablespoonfuls onto foil-lined cookie sheet. Place in preheated oven and turn off heat. Leave cookies inside oven for 8 hours or overnight. Do not peek! Yields 3 dozen.

QUICK AND EASY TOFFEE BARS

12-15 Graham crackers
1 cup butter, melted
1 cup brown sugar

1 12-ounce package
    chocolate chips
1 cup pecans, chopped

Preheat oven to 400 degrees. Line cookie sheet or pan with foil. Place a layer of Graham crackers over the foil. Simmer the butter and brown sugar for 3 minutes, then pour quickly over the Graham crackers. Bake 5 minutes. Remove from oven and sprinkle with nuts and chocolate chips (these may be melted together and poured over if desired). Cool, then refrigerate. Break into pieces when hardened. Keep in refrigerator. Yields 24 pieces.

TOKYO COOKIES

8 tablespoons margarine
2 cups sugar
4 tablespoons cocoa
½ cup milk

2½ cups oats (quick - uncooked)
1 teaspoon vanilla

Bring to a rolling boil the margarine, sugar, cocoa and milk. Boil over medium heat about 10 minutes. Remove from heat. Add oats and vanilla and immediately begin spooning out cookies on wax paper. Let harden. Yields 3 dozen.

The summer I turned 10, we spent two weeks at a ranch near the Gallatin River in Montana. While Dad and the cowboys worked cattle, we kids tubed down Cherry Creek. I made these cookies every afternoon when we finished tubing, 12 days in a row, and we never tired of them. They are GREAT!

HELLO DOLLY BARS

¼ pound (1 stick) butter or margarine
1 cup vanilla wafer or graham cracker crumbs
1 cup flaked coconut

1 cup semi-sweet chocolate chips
1 cup chopped pecans
1 can sweetened condensed milk

Preheat oven to 350 degrees. Melt butter and pour into a 9 x 13 pan. Layer crumbs, coconut, chips and pecans into buttered pan. Pour condensed milk over top. Bake 25-30 minutes. Cool and cut into small squares to serve.

Zana Martin, a bright and beloved eighty-eight year old, finds that these HELLO DOLLY BARS are one of her most-requested desserts at church covered-dish suppers, which are a long-time tradition in East Texas.

PUMPKIN CHEESECAKE BARS

Crust:
1 cup flour
⅓ cup brown sugar, firmly
 packed

5 tablespoons softened
 margarine
½ cup nuts, finely chopped

Filling:
1 8-ounce package cream
 cheese
¾ cup white sugar
½ cup canned pumpkin

2 eggs, slightly beaten
1½ teaspoons cinnamon
1 teaspoon allspice
1 teaspoon vanilla

Preheat oven to 350 degrees. For crust, combine flour and brown sugar and cut butter into mixture until crumbly. Reserve ¾ cup for topping. Press into 8 x 8-inch pan. Bake for 15 minutes. Cool. For filling, combine all ingredients and blend until smooth. Pour over crust. Sprinkle with reserved topping. Bake at 350 degrees for 30 - 35 minutes. Cool before slicing. Yields 16 bars.

CHOCOLATE CHERRY BARS

1 package fudge cake mix
1 21-ounce can cherry fruit
 filling

1 teaspoon almond extract
2 eggs, beaten

Frosting:
1 cup sugar
5 tablespoons butter or
 margarine

⅓ cup milk
1 6-ounce package semi-
 sweet chocolate pieces

Preheat oven to 350 degrees. Butter and flour 15 x 10-inch jelly roll or 13 x 9-inch pan. In large bowl, combine first four ingredients. By hand, stir until well mixed. Pour into prepared pan. If using 15 x 10-inch pan, bake 20 - 30 minutes. If using 13 x 9-inch pan, bake 25 - 30 minutes, or until toothpick inserted in center comes out clean. Frosting: In small saucepan, combine sugar, butter and milk. Boil, stirring constantly for 1 minute. Remove from heat; stir in chocolate pieces until smooth. Pour over chocolate cookie and cut into bars. Yields 3 dozen.

MARY DE LAMAR BROWNIES

1 14-ounce bag caramels
⅔ cup evaporated milk,
  divided use
1 8½-ounce package German
  chocolate cake mix

¾ cup butter, softened
1 cup chopped nuts
  (optional)
1 6-ounce package chocolate
  chips

Combine caramels and ⅓ cup milk in double boiler until caramels are melted. Stir well. Remove from heat and set aside. Combine cake mix, remaining milk and butter, mixing well in mixer. Add nuts, if desired. Press half the cake mixture into buttered 13 x 9-inch baking pan. Bake at 350 degrees for 6 minutes. Sprinkle chocolate chips over crust; pour caramel mixture over chips. Spread. Use remaining cake mixture to cover caramel layer. Return pan to oven and bake 15 - 18 minutes. Cool. Chill for 30 minutes and cut into bars. Yields 24 bars.

FAVORITE BROWNIES

4 eggs
2 cups sugar
1 cup margarine, melted
6 tablespoons cocoa
1½ cups flour

1 teaspoon vanilla
1 12-ounce package Reese's
  Peanut Butter Chips,
  chilled

Preheat oven to 350 degrees. Beat eggs and sugar. Add margarine and cocoa and mix well. Mix together flour, vanilla and peanut butter chips, and add to mixture. Bake in a sprayed 9 x 13-inch pan for 30 minutes. May be cut into large squares and topped with whipped cream.

GINGERSNAPS

2 cups unsalted butter, at
    room temperature
2½ cups dark brown sugar
3 eggs
¾ cup molasses
4½ cups unbleached flour

¼ cup ground ginger
1¼ teaspoons ground
    cinnamon
1½ teaspoons baking soda
½ teaspoon salt

Preheat oven to 325 degrees. Cream butter and brown sugar until light. Beat in eggs, then molasses. Sift flour, ginger, cinnamon, baking soda, and salt into another bowl. Using a wooden spoon, stir liquid mixture into flour mixture until combined. Butter baking pans or line with parchment paper. Drop batter onto pans by the teaspoonful. Press each down with a moistened finger. Bake for 10 to 13 minutes or until lightly browned. DO NOT OVERCOOK. Cool and remove from pan. Yields 5-6 dozen.

STRAWBERRY PATCH COOKIES

1 egg white
1 cup brown sugar
1 tablespoon flour

pinch of salt
1 cup pecans, lightly toasted
    and chopped

Preheat oven to 325 degrees. Beat egg whites to a stiff froth. Add brown sugar and continue beating. Stir in flour, salt and pecans and continue beating. Drop by teaspoonfuls, far apart from each other, on buttered cookie sheet, and bake for 10 minutes. Remove from pan when partly cooled. A tea party cookie. Yields 2 dozen.

BEACON HILL COOKIES

1 cup chocolate chips
2 egg whites
dash of salt
½ cup sugar
½ teaspoon vanilla

½ teaspoon vinegar
¾ cup walnuts, coarsely
    chopped
½ cup coconut

Preheat oven to 350 degrees. Melt chocolate chips in top of double boiler. Beat egg whites with salt until foamy. Gradually add sugar to egg whites, beating until stiff peaks are formed. Stir in vanilla and vinegar. Fold in melted chocolate, coconut and walnuts. Drop onto buttered or sprayed cookie sheets. Bake for 10 minutes. After cooling for a few minutes, remove cookies to a wire rack. Yields 3 dozen.

LEMON BARS

1 cup butter (not margarine)
½ cup powdered sugar
2 cups flour
¼ teaspoon salt
4 beaten eggs
2 cups sugar

¼ cup sifted flour
1 teaspoon finely grated
lemon rind
5 tablespoons fresh lemon
juice

Preheat oven to 350 degrees. Soften butter; blend well with powdered sugar, flour and salt. Press into bottom of a buttered 9 x 13-inch pan. Bake for 20 minutes. Blend together remaining ingredients, mixing beaten eggs with flour, then adding the sugar, lemon rind and lemon juice. Stir and pour over first (baked) layer, and continue baking 25 minutes. Sift additional powdered sugar over top immediately after removing from oven. Cool and cut into squares. Store in refrigerator. Yields 3 dozen.

APRICOT BARS

Pastry Crust:
½ cup butter
¼ cup sugar
1 cup flour

powdered sugar for final
dusting

Filling:
2 eggs
1 cup brown sugar
⅓ cup flour
½ teaspoon baking powder
¼ teaspoon salt
1 teaspoon vanilla

1 teaspoon lemon juice
1 cup dried apricots, chopped,
divided use
1 cup nuts, chopped
¾ cup coconut (optional)

Boil ⅔ cup dried apricots in 1 cup water for 10 minutes. Drain. Chop and set aside. Preheat oven to 325 degrees. For pastry, mix butter, sugar and flour. Press into 9 x 13-inch pan and bake for 20 - 25 minutes. For filling, beat eggs and gradually add brown sugar. Stir in dry ingredients. Add vanilla and lemon juice. Fold in apricots and nuts. Pour over the baked pastry and bake an additional 20 minutes. Cool and dust with powdered sugar. Cut into squares. Yields 2½ dozen squares.

CARAMELS

6 cups granulated sugar
½ pound butter
2 cups dark Karo syrup (blue
    label bottle)

2 cups cream
½ pound pecans, toasted

Put sugar, butter, Karo and ½ of cream in heavy pan. When it comes to a full boil, add remainder of cream slowly and stir. Simmer and stir until candy thermometer reaches 242 - 245 degrees. Be careful and do not scorch. Add pecans. Pour onto buttered 9 x 12-inch pan. Cool and slice. This recipe is best made with a gas flame. Yields 24 - 36 pieces.

PEANUT BRITTLE

2 cups raw, peeled peanuts
1 cup sugar
½ cup Karo syrup

½ cup water
2 teaspoons baking soda

Butter cookie sheet. Add together in large pot peanuts, sugar, Karo and water. Cook on high (heavy boil) for 9 minutes, stirring constantly after first 5 minutes. Add baking soda and stir. Remove from stove immediately. Stir, turn out on cookie sheet and spread. When cooled, break into pieces. Yields 24 - 36 pieces.

GLAZED WALNUTS

½ cup butter
1 cup brown sugar

1 teaspoon cinnamon
4 cups walnuts

Microwave butter 1 minute on high. Add brown sugar and cinnamon, and cook 2 minutes on high. Add walnuts and cook 3 to 5 minutes on high. Pour onto wax paper/separate nuts. (Cook in 1½-quart glass dish.) Yields 4 cups.

HOLIDAY ICEBOX ROLL

1 box vanilla wafers
1 cup candied red cherries
1 cup candied green cherries
1 cup candied pineapple

1 cup condensed milk
2 cups pecans, cut up
powdered sugar

Crush wafers into fine crumbs. Cut all fruit in half; pineapple in pieces. Mix all together. Roll into small logs and then roll in powdered sugar. Wrap in wax paper and chill. Cut and serve. Yields 36 slices.

CARAMEL CANDIED POPCORN

4 quarts freshly popped corn, unsalted
½ cup raw peanuts
2 cups pecans
1 cup margarine
2 cups light brown sugar, firmly packed

½ cup light corn syrup
½ teaspoon baking soda
½ teaspoon salt
1 teaspoon vanilla
1½ teaspoons butter flavoring

Preheat oven to 250 degrees. Combine popcorn, peanuts and pecans in lightly buttered roasting pan and set aside. Melt margarine in large saucepan. Stir in sugar and corn syrup. Bring to a slow boil and boil 5 minutes, stirring occasionally. Remove from heat, stir in flavorings, salt and soda. Pour sugar mixture over popcorn mixture, stirring until evenly coated. Bake for 1 hour, stirring every 15 minutes. Cool and store in airtight container. Yields 5 quarts.

WHITE CHOCOLATE KRISPIES

1 pound white chocolate, melted
2½ cups Rice Krispies

1 12-ounce jar dry roasted peanuts

Mix together. Drop by spoonfuls on wax paper. Yields 2 - 3 dozen.

TOFFEE CANDY

1 cup toasted nuts, chopped
1 cup butter
1 cup sugar
1 tablespoon water

3 tablespoons dark Karo
   syrup
7-8 plain Hershey chocolate
   bars, or Hershey milk
   chocolate chips

Spread 1 cup chopped, toasted nuts on a 9 x 12-inch unbuttered pan. In a heavy pan, stir together butter, sugar, water and Karo syrup, and cook on medium heat (on top of stove). Stir until mixture changes to a darker color, and a small drop becomes brittle when dropped into cold water. Pour hot mixture over nuts. Cover mixture with 7 to 8 plain Hershey bars or with milk chocolate chips. When chocolate has melted, smooth with a knife. Place in refrigerator. When cooled, break into pieces to serve. Yields 20 pieces.

DATE LOAF

4 cups sugar
2 heaping tablespoons flour
14 dates, cut up
1¾ small cans evaporated
   milk

8 tablespoons butter
1 teaspoon vanilla
1½ cups (or more) toasted
   pecans, chopped

Using a heavy pan, mix sugar, flour, dates and milk with a wooden spoon. Place on heat and cook over medium flame, stirring constantly so that the candy will not scorch. Cook until it forms a hard ball in cold water (265 degrees on candy thermometer). Remove from heat and add butter, vanilla and pecans. Set the pan in cold water and beat until candy begins to stiffen. Pour out on dampened cloth and shape into a loaf, or roll, using cloth to shape. Refrigerate until cool. Wrap in wax paper, then foil. Slice to serve. Yields 24-36 pieces.

ROCKY ROAD FUDGE

Bar:

½ cup margarine
1 1-ounce square
   unsweetened chocolate
1 cup sugar
1 cup all-purpose flour

½ cup chopped nuts
   (optional)
1 teaspoon baking powder
1 teaspoon vanilla
2 eggs

Filling:

8 ounces cream cheese,
   softened (reserve 2
   ounces for frosting)
½ cup sugar
2 tablespoons flour
¼ cup margarine, softened

1 egg
½ teaspoon vanilla
¼ cup nuts (optional)
1 6-ounce package (1 cup)
   semi-sweet chocolate
   chips

Frosting:

2 cups miniature
   marshmallows
¼ cup margarine
1 1-ounce square
   unsweetened chocolate

2 ounces cream cheese (from
   reserve)
¼ cup milk
3 cups powdered sugar
1 teaspoon vanilla

Preheat oven to 350 degrees. Butter and flour a 13 x 9-inch pan. In large saucepan over low heat melt ½ cup margarine and 1 square chocolate. Add remaining Bar ingredients and mix well. Spread in prepared pan. Cool. In a small bowl combine 6 ounces cream cheese with next 5 Filling ingredients. Beat 1 minute at medium speed until smooth, and stir in nuts. Spread over chocolate mixture. Sprinkle with chocolate chips. Bake at 350 degrees for 25 to 30 minutes. Remove and sprinkle with marshmallows. Bake 2 minutes longer. In saucepan over low heat melt ¼ cup margarine, 1 square chocolate, 2 ounces cream cheese and milk. Stir in powdered sugar and vanilla until smooth. Immediately pour over marshmallows and swirl together. Cool. Cut into bars and store in refrigerator. Makes 3-4 dozen.

DOUBLE PEANUT FUDGE

2 cups sugar
⅔ cup milk
1 cup marshmallow creme
1 cup creamy peanut butter

1 6-ounce package semi-
  sweet chocolate morsels
1 teaspoon vanilla
½ cup roasted peanuts,
  coarsely chopped

Combine sugar and milk in a heavy saucepan. Cook over medium heat, stirring until mixture reaches soft ball stage (234 degrees with candy thermometer). Remove from heat. Add next 4 ingredients. Stir until mixture is well blended and then fold in peanuts. Pour into a buttered 8-inch square pan. Cool and cut into squares. Yields 2 dozen.

NEW ORLEANS PRALINES

½ cup unsalted butter
1 cup heavy cream
2 cups granulated sugar

2¼ cups brown sugar, packed
1 pound pecans, toasted and
  coarsely chopped

Spread sheets of wax paper on 2 large baking sheets. In a heavy saucepan over high heat, combine butter, cream and sugars. Bring to boil, then stir in pecans. Return mixture to boil, then remove from heat. Drop praline mixture from a soup spoon to make 1½-inch circles. Work quickly! Let stand 6 hours at room temperature, then store in airtight container. Yields 5 dozen.

UNBELIEVABLY EASY MICROWAVE PRALINES

1 cup whipping cream
1 pound light brown sugar
2 cups pecan halves, toasted

2 tablespoons margarine at
  room temperature
  (important)

Mix cream and brown sugar together in large (3½- to 4-quart) glass bowl. Plastic will not work as well. Microwave on high for 13½ minutes. Do NOT stop to stir, even though it may smell like it's burning! Quickly add pecans and margarine, stirring until all margarine is mixed in. Drop on unbuttered foil (works better than wax paper). Makes about 35.

Desserts

Texas Rose Festival

Young and old alike participate in the
Texas Rose Festival where the Rose Queen
holds court with thousands of visitors
each October. The Queen's Tea offers a
bounty of desserts and beverages amid
ten thousand "dozen" roses featured in
mirrors, walkways and fountains. The
Rose Festival culminates in the pageantry
of the Queen's Coronation. The final day is
celebrated with a spectacular parade
showcasing a myriad of magical floats.

Festival weekend visitors tour the Tyler
Rose Garden which is the world's largest,
with 500 varieties of the rose and more
than 30,000 bushes. Bus tours of nearby
rose fields are also a popular attraction.

BERRY-BERRY MOUSSE IN A CAKE ROLL

Cakes:
4 large eggs
½ cup water

1 18½-ounce package cake mix

Berry-Berry Mousse:
1 envelope unflavored gelatin
2 tablespoons cold water
juice of 1 lemon
grated zest of 1 lemon
2 cups frozen raspberries (or fresh if available)

2 cups frozen strawberries (or fresh if available)
2 tablespoons crème de cassis
2 egg yolks
½ cup sugar
2 cups whipping cream
mint sprigs for garnish

Preheat oven to 350 degrees. Coat 2 (15 x 10 x 1-inch) jellyroll pans with cooking spray. Line with wax paper. Coat again with spray. Set aside. Beat eggs for 5 minutes. Add water and gradually add cake mix. Beat until moistened. Divide batter in half, and spread evenly into prepared pans (layers will be thin). Bake at 350 degrees for about 13 minutes in middle rack of oven. Turn cooked cakes out onto a sugared towel. Peel off wax paper. Starting at narrow end, roll up each cake and towel together. Set aside to cool. **To Make Mousse:** Combine gelatin and water in saucepan and soak for 5 minutes. Stir lemon juice into gelatin. Add zest, raspberries, strawberries and crème de cassis. Boil and stir frequently until thick. Set aside to cool. Combine egg yolks and sugar and beat until pale yellow. Simmer over low heat, whisking often, until hot and slightly thickened, 10 to 15 minutes. Set aside custard to cool. When cool, fold berry mixture into custard. Whip cream until soft peaks form. Gently fold into custard-berry mixture. Spread mousse over each cake layer and roll up. Store seam side down. Slice to serve on plate garnished with raspberries (or raspberry sauce) and mint. Serves 12-14. A beautiful dinner party dessert. (**Raspberry Sauce,** see page 66.)

Tyler Rose Museum, located at the Tyler Rose Garden, is open to visitors year around and showcases royalty gowns, historical films, pageant photographs and memorabilia.

BOILED CUSTARD

½ gallon milk (8 cups)   pinch of salt
7 eggs   1 teaspoon vanilla
8½ tablespoons sugar

Heat milk in double boiler or over low heat in a heavy saucepan. Beat eggs, sugar and salt in a separate bowl. Gradually add to heated milk, stirring constantly until mixture coats a spoon. Add vanilla and serve hot or cold. Sprinkle with grated nutmeg. Yields 2 quarts.

TIRAMISU

1 10¾-ounce package frozen   ⅔ cup superfine sugar
   pound cake, thawed, or   2 tablespoons brandy
   lady fingers   ½ teaspoon vanilla extract
8 ounces mascarpone cheese,   ½ cup espresso or strong
   or cream cheese   coffee
1½ cups heavy cream   unsweetened cocoa powder

With electric knife, trim dark top from cake and discard. Cut cake horizontally into 4 equal layers. With 2½-inch cutter, cut out 3 rounds from each layer; break remaining cake into large crumbs. In small bowl of electric mixer, at medium speed, beat mascarpone with heavy cream and ½ cup sugar until soft peaks form when beaters are raised. Beat in 1 tablespoon brandy and the vanilla until stiff. In cup, combine coffee with remaining brandy and sugar, stirring until sugar dissolves. Place a spoonful of cheese mixture in each of 6 large wine glasses; top each with a cake round. Brush cake rounds with some coffee mixture. Top cake in each glass with a spoonful of remaining cheese mixture, spreading mixture to edge of glass; sprinkle each with cake crumbs, dividing evenly, and sprinkle cake with some coffee mixture. Repeat layering in each glass: cheese mixture, cake round and remaining coffee mixture; spoon remaining cheese mixture over all. Dust with cocoa powder. Refrigerate at least 1 hour; remove from refrigerator 30 minutes before serving. If desired, serve with chocolate candy sticks. Serves 6.

Variation: Layer ⅓ cheese mixture in loaf pan, cover with horizontal cake slice. Brush cake with coffee, brandy, and sugar mixture. Add another layer of cheese, then cake which is brushed again with coffee mixture. Continue to use all cake, cheese and coffee. Refrigerate 1-2 hours. Unmold and slice to serve.

CHOCOLATE MOUSSE ANGEL PIE

Meringue Crust:
4 egg whites, at room temperature

pinch of cream of tartar
1 cup sugar

Chocolate Mousse Filling:
5 eggs, separated, at room temperature
¼ teaspoon cream of tartar
1 cup sugar
⅛ teaspoon salt
2 teaspoons lemon juice

4 ounces (4 squares) unsweetened chocolate, melted and cooled to room temperature)
1⅔ cups heavy cream

Garnish:
chocolate curls (optional)

Meringue Crust: Preheat oven to 325 degrees. Spray a 10-inch pie pan with vegetable spray. In a large bowl, beat egg whites until foamy. Add cream of tartar. Gradually, add sugar and continue to beat until stiff peaks form. Pour meringue into prepared pie pan and bake for 45 minutes until puffed and cracked. Remove meringue from oven and set aside to cool. During cooling, the center of crust will fall. Chocolate Mousse Filling: In a large bowl, beat egg whites with cream of tartar until soft peaks form. Two tablespoons at a time, add ¾ cup of the sugar; beat well after each addition. Continue beating until stiff peaks form. In a medium bowl, beat egg yolks with salt until thick and lemon colored. Gradually add remaining sugar, beating well. Slowly add lemon juice, melted chocolate and ⅓ cup of the heavy cream. Beat until mixture is smooth and thickened. In a small bowl, beat remaining heavy cream until stiff. Add whipped cream and chocolate mixture to egg whites and carefully fold them together. Pour mousse into cooled meringue crust. Refrigerate overnight until set. Garnish with chocolate curls. Serves 8.

CHOCOLATE MOUSSE CAKE

4 ounces semi-sweet baking
  chocolate
½ cup unsalted butter, cut
  into small pieces

4 egg yolks
½ cup granulated sugar
3 egg whites

Icing:
4 ounces unsweetened
  chocolate
½ cup unsalted butter, cut
  into small pieces

4 egg yolks
½ cup sugar
3 egg whites

Preheat oven to 325 degrees. Butter bottom and sides of an 8-inch springform pan. Combine chocolate and ½ cup butter in double boiler. Simmer over water, stirring frequently, until melted. Remove from heat and let cool. Beat egg yolks and sugar in a large bowl until light and lemon-colored. Add chocolate mixture, blend well. Beat egg whites in a medium bowl until stiff peaks form. Stir half of egg white mixture into chocolate mixture; fold in remaining whites. Pour batter into prepared pan. Bake 1 hour. Remove to a wire rack. Cool 15 minutes. Remove sides and invert onto a serving plate. While cake is cooling, make icing: Combine chocolate and butter in top of double boiler. Simmer until chocolate melts. Remove from heat. Beat egg yolks and sugar in a large bowl. Add cooled chocolate mixture and blend well. Beat egg whites in medium bowl until soft peaks form. Beat half the egg whites into chocolate mixture. Fold in remaining whites. Use immediately. Spread icing over top and sides of cake. Best if made a day or two early and put into refrigerator to mellow. Serves 8.

Toasting nuts: Many of our recipes require toasted nuts. Careful cooks have discovered that toasting nuts before adding to recipes brings out their flavor and aroma. Spread nuts, whole or cut up, in a single layer on a baking sheet and toast in a preheated 350 degree oven until fragrant and golden brown, 3 to 5 minutes. Stir nuts once or twice as they cook so they brown evenly. Check at 3 minutes to see if they have begun to color. After this point, they toast quickly so watch carefully so as to not let them burn. To plan ahead: Toast nuts as you buy them. Then store or freeze in a plastic bag for ready use.

CHOCOLATE MOUSSE

2 cups semi-sweet chocolate
  chips
1½ teaspoons vanilla
pinch of salt

1½ cups whipping cream,
  scalded
6 egg yolks
whipped cream for topping

Combine chocolate chips, vanilla and salt in food processor (steel knife), and mix 30 seconds. Add scalded cream and continue mixing 30 seconds more, or until chocolate is completely melted. Add yolks and mix 5 seconds. Transfer to a bowl and cool. Beat egg whites until stiff peaks form. Gently fold into chocolate mixture. Place in glasses or bowl, and cover with plastic wrap. Chill. Serves 4-6.

CHOCOLATE CHIP CHEESECAKE

15-20 Oreo or Hydrox
  cookies, crushed
24 ounces cream cheese,
  softened
1 can sweetened condensed
  milk
3 eggs
2 teaspoons vanilla

½ cup mini chocolate chips
2 teaspoons flour
whipped cream for garnish
chocolate shavings for
  garnish
strawberries or cherries for
  garnish

Preheat oven to 300 degrees. Blend cream cheese, milk, eggs and vanilla until smooth. Toss chocolate chips with flour and fold into cream cheese mixture. In a food processor, crush cookies until fine. Line bottom of springform pan with crushed cookies. Pour cheesecake batter over crust. Sprinkle a few more chocolate chips on top, if desired. Bake for 1 hour or until set. Garnish after chilling (2 hours or more) with whipped cream, chocolate shavings and a strawberry or cherry. Serves 8-10.

LEMON GLAZED CHEESECAKE

2 cups graham cracker
    crumbs
6 tablespoons butter, melted
2 tablespoons sugar
3 8-ounce packages cream
    cheese
¾ cup sugar
3 eggs
¼ cup lemon juice

2 teaspoons grated lemon
    rind
2 teaspoons vanilla
2 cups sour cream
3 tablespoons sugar
1 teaspoon vanilla
mint leaves for garnish
strawberries for garnish

Lemon Glaze:
½ cup sugar
1½ tablespoons cornstarch
¼ teaspoon salt
¾ cup water

⅓ cup lemon juice
1 egg yolk
1 tablespoon water
1 teaspoon grated lemon rind

Preheat oven to 350 degrees. Combine first 3 ingredients. Press crust into bottom and sides of buttered 9 x 3-inch springform pan. Bake 5 minutes. Cool. Beat cream cheese until soft. Add sugar, blending thoroughly. Add eggs 1 at a time, beating well after each addition. Mix in lemon juice, rind and vanilla. Blend well. Pour into springform pan. Bake 35 minutes. While cake is baking, blend sour cream, sugar and vanilla. Remove cake from oven. Gently spread sour cream mixture over top. Return to oven and bake 12 minutes. Cool for 30 minutes on a rack. Lemon Glaze: In heavy saucepan mix sugar, cornstarch and salt. Combine water, lemon juice and egg yolk and add to sugar mixture. Cook over low heat, stirring constantly, until mixture comes to a slow boil and is thickened. Add butter and lemon rind. Allow to cool slightly, but spread on cheesecake before glaze sets. Chill cheesecake several hours, or overnight before removing side of pan. Garnish with mint leaves and strawberries.

CHOCOLATE-RASPBERRY TRUFFLE CHEESECAKE

2½ cups chocolate wafer
   crumbs
⅓ cup butter, melted
½ cup sugar
1 8-ounce package semi-
   sweet chocolate squares,
   cut into ½-inch cubes
½ cup strong hot coffee
3 8-ounce packages cream
   cheese, cut into 1-inch
   cubes

1 8-ounce carton sour cream
1 cup sugar
2 eggs
2 tablespoons whipping
   cream
1 teaspoon vanilla extract
¼ cup chambord (raspberry
   liqueur)
whipped cream for garnish
mint sprigs for garnish
raspberry (below) for serving
   sauce

Raspberry Sauce:
1 10-ounce package frozen
   raspberries, thawed
2 teaspoons cornstarch

¼ cup triple sec, or any
   orange liqueur

Raspberry sauce: combine ingredients and cook on top of stove until thickened. Cheesecake: Combine first 3 ingredients; blend well. Press on bottom and 1½ inches up sides of 9-inch springform pan. Set aside. Position knife blade in food processor bowl, add chocolate cubes and process until finely ground. With food processor running, pour hot coffee, and process until chocolate is melted and smooth. Add cream cheese and next 6 ingredients; process until smooth, stopping once to scrape sides of bowl. Pour mixture into prepared crust and bake for 55 minutes at 350 degrees (center will be soft). Let cool to room temperature on a wire rack. Cover and chill at least 8 hours. Remove from pan. Serve on a pool of raspberry sauce, and garnish as desired.

CARAMEL PECAN PIE

28 caramels
¼ cup water
¼ cup butter
¾ cup sugar

2 eggs, slightly beaten
¼ teaspoon salt
½ teaspoon vanilla
1 cup pecans

Preheat oven to 400 degrees. Melt caramels with water in microwave. Add remaining ingredients and pour into unbaked pie shell which has been prebaked 6 minutes at 400 degrees before adding filling. Bake for 10 minutes, then lower temperature to 350 degrees for 20 minutes, or until done. Serves 8.

CHOCOLATE MACADAMIA NUT PIE

6 ounces chocolate wafers,
  crushed (1⅔ cups)
4 tablespoons butter, melted
6 ounces semi-sweet
  chocolate
4 ounces cream cheese,
  softened

¾ cup sugar
1½ teaspoons vanilla
1 3½-ounce jar macadamia
  nuts, coarsely chopped
2 cups whipping cream

Crush wafers in food processor. Combine crumbs with melted butter and press into bottom of 9-inch springform pan. Melt chocolate in double boiler over hot water. Allow to cool slightly. Beat together melted chocolate, cream cheese, sugar and vanilla. Fold nuts into creamed mixture. Whip cream until peaks form. Beat about ¼ of whipped cream into cheese mixture. Gently fold in remaining cream. Pour filling into crumb crust. Freeze 4 hours, or overnight. Remove from freezer 10 minutes before serving. Serves 10.

ORANGE SHERBET PIE

½ cup butter
1 7-ounce package flaked
  coconut

1 half-gallon orange sherbet,
  softened
1 to 2 tablespoons orange
  liqueur (optional)

Melt butter in large skillet over medium heat. Add coconut and cook, stirring constantly, until golden, about 6-7 minutes. Remove from heat. Reserve 2 tablespoons coconut for garnish. Press remainder into bottom and sides of a 9-inch pie plate. Spread half of orange sherbet over crust. Drizzle with liqueur. Add remaining sherbet, mounding top. Sprinkle with reserved coconut. Freeze until ready to serve or overnight. Let stand about 10 minutes before slicing. May be made days ahead. Great in spring or summer. Serves 8-10.

BUTTERMILK PIE

pastry for 9-inch pie, unbaked
3 large eggs
¾ cup sugar
3 tablespoons all-purpose
  flour
1½ cups buttermilk
¾ teaspoon pure vanilla
  extract
3 tablespoons fresh lemon
  juice
1 teaspoon grated lemon rind
1 tablespoon unsalted butter,
  melted
½ teaspoon ground nutmeg

Preheat oven to 375 degrees. Cover unbaked pie crust with parchment paper. Place crust in preheated oven and bake for 10 minutes. Remove from oven. Beat eggs and sugar until light and lemon colored. Add flour and beat until well mixed. Add buttermilk, vanilla, lemon juice, lemon rind and butter. Pour into partially baked crust and dust with nutmeg. Bake 25 - 30 additional minutes. Cool slightly on wire rack before serving. **To partially bake pie crust:** Bake for 10 minutes at 375 degrees. Remove from oven, and then add moist fillings.

FAMOUS POTATO PIE

4 medium sized sweet
  potatoes (about 1
  pound)
¼ cup butter or margarine
2 tablespoons undiluted
  evaporated milk
¼ cup white corn syrup
2 eggs, beaten
1¼ to 1½ cups brown sugar
1 teaspoon nutmeg
½ teaspoon cinnamon
¼ teaspoon cloves
¼ teaspoon salt
1 9-inch partially pre-baked
  pie crust (pre-bake for 10
  minutes at 375 degrees
  before adding potato
  filling)

Preheat oven to 350 degrees. Place unpeeled sweet potatoes in a kettle. Cover with water and cook, covered, for 25-30 minutes over high heat. The potatoes should be soft to the touch when done. Pour off hot water, replacing with cold water. As soon as potatoes are cool enough to handle, peel by hand under cold running water. Skin should slip off easily. Place potatoes in a medium sized mixing bowl. Mash lightly; add butter, evaporated milk, corn syrup, eggs, sugar and spices. Blend with mixer at medium speed until smooth. Pour filling into partially baked crust. Bake for 35 to 45 minutes, or until filling is lightly browned. Do not over-bake or filling will be dry. Delicious when served warm. Serves 8-10.

APPLE CRUMB PIE

1 Pillsbury All Ready Pie
   Crust (red box)
5 apples (Delicious), peeled
   and sliced small (7 cups)
1 tablespoon lemon juice
½ teaspoon vanilla

1 heaping tablespoon flour
¼ cup brown sugar
½ cup sugar
less than ⅛ teaspoon cloves
dots of margarine

Topping:
8 tablespoons margarine,
   melted

⅔ cup sugar
1 cup flour

Prepare pie crust according to directions and place in a 9-inch foil pan. Flute edges of pie crust as desired. Peel and slice apples into a large bowl. Add remainder of ingredients, stirring well until some juice appears and apples are well coated. Spoon into pie crust and dot with margarine. Preheat oven to 450 degrees. Topping: Melt margarine and stir in sugar and flour. Mix by hand until well blended. Take portions of this mixture and flatten by hand, placing on top of apples until all of pie is covered. May be frozen at this point, unbaked. But if baking, place pie on cookie sheet. Bake 15 minutes. Reduce heat to 325 degrees and bake 35 minutes. Excellent for freezing. To prepare frozen pie: DO NOT THAW. Preheat oven to 450 degrees. Place pie on cookie sheet. Bake for 15 minutes. Reduce heat to 300-325 degrees and bake 1½ hours longer. If apples other than Delicious are used, increase sugar amount. Serves 8.

BLUEBERRY CRUMB PIE

1 9-inch pie shell, partially
   pre baked
3 cups fresh blueberries
¾ cup sugar

1 tablespoon flour
pinch of salt
¼ teaspoon lemon zest

Crumb Topping:
¾ cup fine dry cookie crumbs
¼ cup flour
1 teaspoon cinnamon

⅛ teaspoon nutmeg
¼ cup softened margarine

Preheat oven to 450 degrees. Fill shell with blueberries. Mix together sugar, flour, salt and lemon zest. Sprinkle mixture on blueberries. Bake 10 minutes. Mix together crumb topping ingredients and cover pie with crumbs. Reduce oven to 350 degrees and continue to bake for 30 - 40 minutes. Serves 6-8.

FRESH STRAWBERRY PIE

1 baked 9-inch pie shell
2 pints fresh strawberries
3 tablespoons cornstarch
⅛ teaspoon salt
1 cup sugar

1 teaspoon lemon juice
1 cup heavy cream, whipped
powdered sugar
vanilla

Wash and dry strawberries. Remove stems. Arrange largest berries on bottom of pie shell, tips pointing up. Use enough to cover bottom of shell. Mix cornstarch, salt and sugar. Add remaining strawberries, mashed. Cook over medium heat until thick. Cool after adding lemon juice. Pour over strawberries. Refrigerate until firm. Sweeten cream with powdered sugar. Add vanilla to taste and spread on top. Serves 8.

MERINGUE SHELLS (BASIC MERINGUE)

1 cup egg whites at room
     temperature (8 to 10
     whites)
½ teaspoon cream of tartar
¼ teaspoon salt

1 teaspoon vanilla extract,
     or ½ teaspoon almond
     extract
2 cups extra fine sugar

Beat egg whites until frothy. Add cream of tartar, salt and vanilla. Beat until soft peaks form. Add sugar, 1 tablespoon at a time, continually beating until stiff peaks form. Preheat oven to 250 degrees. Spoon meringues by tablespoonfuls onto a well-sprayed cookie sheet. Shape into shells with back of spoon. Bake 1 hour. Allow to cool thoroughly before removing from pan with a spatula. Baked meringues may be stored in an airtight container. Serve with fresh fruit and whipped cream. Yields 10 to 12 meringues.

Meringue Tips:
- *Bowl, beaters, and hands should be dry and oil-free.*
- *Eggs separate best when cold, but beat best at room temperature.*
- *Beat the meringue until shiny and very stiff but not dry. If underbeaten, the meringue will weep. If overbeaten, the meringue will clump together instead of spreading evenly. Then it will bake flat with beads of sugar on top.*

PEACH COBBLER SUPREME

8 cups sliced fresh peaches
1¾ cups sugar
1 teaspoon almond extract
2-4 tablespoons flour

½ teaspoon ground nutmeg
⅓ cup butter, melted
pastry for double-crust pie

Preheat oven to 475 degrees. Combine peaches, sugar, flour and nutmeg. Set aside until syrup forms. Bring to a boil. Cook over low heat 10 minutes, or until tender. Remove from heat; add almond extract and butter, stirring well. Roll one-half of pastry to ⅛-inch thickness on floured surface, and cut into 10 x 8-inch rectangle. Spoon half the peach mixture into a lightly buttered 10 x 8-inch baking dish, then top with pastry. Bake 10 minutes or until pastry is golden brown. Spoon remaining peaches over baked pastry. Roll remaining pastry and cut into ½-inch strips. Arrange in lattice design over peaches. Return to oven for 10-15 minutes, or until browned.

HOT FUDGE PUDDING

1 cup flour
¾ cup sugar
2 tablespoons cocoa
2 teaspoons baking powder
¼ teaspoon salt
½ cup milk

2 tablespoons oil
1 cup chopped nuts, toasted
1 cup brown sugar
¼ cup cocoa
1¾ cups hot water
1 teaspoon vanilla

Preheat oven to 350 degrees. Measure flour, sugar, 2 tablespoons cocoa, baking powder and salt in a bowl. Blend in milk and oil; stir in nuts. Pour into unbuttered 9 x 9 x 2-inch pan. Stir together brown sugar and cocoa. Sprinkle over batter. Add vanilla to hot water. Pour over batter. Bake 45 minutes. While hot cut into squares. Put into dish and spoon chocolate sauce over each serving, or if desired, serve with sweetened whipped cream or ice cream. Serves 9.

SHERRY CAKE

4 egg yolks
½ cup sherry
½ cup sugar
1 envelope plain gelatin
⅓ cup milk
4 egg whites

½ pint heavy whipping cream
1 cup sugar
1 medium angel food cake
½ pint unsweetened whipped cream
almonds, toasted and ground

Separate yolks and whites of eggs. Beat yolks, sherry and ½ cup sugar. Cook over medium heat until like a custard. Soak gelatin in milk and stir into hot sherry custard. Let custard cool. Whip egg whites stiff. Whip ½ pint cream with 1 cup sugar. Fold these three into **cooled** custard. Crumble angel food cake. Fold crumbs into egg white/custard mixture until cake is thoroughly moistened. Pour into an oiled 9-inch springform pan. Let stand 8 to 10 hours in refrigerator. Turn out and ice with ½ pint whipped cream. Dust top of cake with toasted almonds. Variations: 1. In place of sherry, use orange liqueur, and add grated orange rind to custard. 2. In place of sherry use **very strong** coffee. Fold toasted, ground almonds into cake/custard mixture. Yields 8-10 slices.

CARROT CAKE

4 eggs
2 cups sugar
1½ cups canola oil
3 cups grated carrots
1 cup nuts, toasted and
    chopped

2 cups flour
2 teaspoons baking soda
1 teaspoon salt
2 teaspoons cinnamon

Frosting:
1 8-ounce package cream
    cheese

4 tablespoons butter
1 box powdered sugar

Preheat oven to 350 degrees. Cream sugar and eggs. Add oil, carrots and nuts. Add sifted dry ingredients. Bake in 9 x 12-inch oiled pan for 25 to 30 minutes. To make frosting, cream the cream cheese and butter together. Add sugar and beat well, until of spreading consistency. Spread on cooled cake.

BABA AU RHUM

Baba Cake:

1½ cups sugar
2 eggs
2 tablespoons heavy cream
⅛ teaspoon salt

1 cup plus 2 heaping
    tablespoons sifted flour
1½ teaspoons baking powder
1 teaspoon vanilla
½ cup hot milk

Sauce:

1½ cups sugar
1 cup cold water

⅓ cup rum (or 2 teaspoons
    rum flavoring)

Topping:

½ pint whipping cream
⅓ cup sugar

1½ teaspoons almond
    flavoring
chopped nuts

Sauce: Boil sugar and water for 3 minutes. Cool. Add rum and let stand. Baba Cake: Preheat oven to 360 degrees. Mix sugar, eggs, heavy cream and salt until smooth. Add flour and baking powder. Add vanilla. Mix in hot milk and pour immediately into buttered pan. Bake 30 minutes. Remove cake from pan onto platter and let cool until warm but not steaming. Pierce cake with fork and pour sauce over cake, letting it soak in. Cover with wax paper and let stand overnight. Topping: Whip ingredients until stiff and ice Baba cake. Fabulous! Serves 20.

SWEDISH PEPPER CAKE

1 cup margarine
1 box dark brown sugar
2 eggs
2 cups flour
1 teaspoon soda

1 teaspoon cinnamon
½ teaspoon ground ginger
½ teaspoon ground cloves
¾ cup sour cream

Preheat oven to 350 degrees. Cream margarine and brown sugar. Add eggs. In a separate bowl, sift together flour, soda, cinnamon, ginger and cloves. Add flour mixture to creamed mixture, then add sour cream. Bake 45 minutes. Cool in pan on rack for 5-10 minutes. Optional: May sprinkle with powdered sugar.

PUMPKIN CAKE ROLL

3 eggs
1 cup sugar
⅔ cup pumpkin
1 teaspoon lemon juice
¾ cup flour
1 teaspoon baking powder
2 teaspoons cinnamon

1 teaspoon ginger
½ teaspoon nutmeg
½ teaspoon salt
1 cup toasted walnuts or
    pecans, finely chopped
powdered sugar

Filling:
1 cup powdered sugar
2 3-ounce packages cream
    cheese

4 tablespoons butter or
    margarine
½ teaspoon vanilla

Preheat oven to 375 degrees. Beat eggs on high speed of mixer for 5 minutes; gradually beat in sugar. Stir in pumpkin and lemon juice. Stir together flour, baking powder, cinnamon, ginger, nutmeg and salt. Fold into pumpkin mixture. Spread into a buttered and floured 15 x 10 x 1-inch pan. Top with nuts. Bake for 15 minutes. Turn out on towel sprinkled with powdered sugar. Starting at the narrow end, roll towel and cake together; cool. Unroll. Beat filling ingredients together until smooth. Spread over cake and roll. Chill. Slice to serve. Serves 8-10.

COCONUT CAKE

1 box yellow cake mix
1 cup sugar
1 pint sour cream

2 7-ounce packages frozen
    fresh coconut
12 ounces Cool Whip

Bake cake according to package directions, in 2 layers. Slice each layer in half, making 4 layers altogether. Combine sugar, sour cream and coconut. Put mixture between each layer of cake, reserving 1 cup. Mix reserved cup with Cool Whip. Ice cake with this mixture. Put in covered cake tin. Refrigerate for 3 days. Do not peek! Serves 10.

PINEAPPLE UPSIDE DOWN CAKE

¼ cup butter
½ cup brown sugar

pineapple slices, drained
Maraschino cherries

Batter:
¼ cup shortening
¾ cup sugar
1 egg, beaten
1¼ cups cake flour

1½ teaspoons baking powder
¼ teaspoon salt
½ cup milk
1 teaspoon vanilla

Preheat oven to 350 degrees. Melt butter and sugar in heavy black skillet. Over sugar, butter mixture arrange drained pineapple slices in a single layer with a cherry in the center of each slice. To make batter, cream shortening. Add sugar gradually and cream until light and fluffy. Add egg and beat thoroughly. Sift flour, baking powder and salt. Add flour alternating with milk to cream mixture, adding flour first and last. Beat after each addition. Add vanilla and pour over pineapples. Bake about 50 minutes. Turn out while still warm. Serves 8.

FRESH APPLE CAKE

1½ cups vegetable oil
2 cups sugar
2 eggs
1 tablespoon vanilla
4 cups fresh apples, diced
   small
1 cup pecans, toasted and
   broken

3 cups flour
½ teaspoon salt
1 teaspoon cinnamon
½ teaspoon ground cloves
½ teaspoon ground nutmeg
1½ teaspoons soda

Preheat oven to 325 degrees. Beat oil, eggs and sugar thoroughly. Add vanilla. Sift spices, salt and soda together. Add to first mixture. Blend well. Fold in apples and nuts. Bake in generously buttered and floured tube pan for 1½ hours. Cool before removing from pan. Yields 1 cake, 2 large loaves or 3 small loaves.

TEXAS CHOCOLATE SHEET CAKE

½ cup butter
½ cup solid shortening
4 tablespoons powdered cocoa
1 cup water
2 cups flour
2 cups sugar

½ cup buttermilk
2 eggs, slightly beaten
1 teaspoon salt
1 teaspoon baking soda
1 teaspoon cinnamon
1 teaspoon vanilla

Icing:
4 tablespoons powdered cocoa
3½ cups powdered sugar
    (1 box), sifted
½ cup butter at room
    temperature

6 tablespoons milk
1 teaspoon vanilla
1 cup pecans, toasted and
    chopped

Preheat oven to 350 degrees. In a saucepan, combine butter, shortening, cocoa and water and bring to a boil. Immediately add flour, sugar, buttermilk, eggs, salt, baking soda, cinnamon and vanilla. Pour into a greased and floured 10 x 15 x 1-inch pan and bake for 22 minutes. Ovens will vary. Cake should be moist. While cake is baking, make icing: Mix cocoa and sugar well. Add milk, vanilla and butter and mix well. Add pecans and stir. Spread icing on cake the minute you remove it from oven. Yields 1 cake.

ABBOT ACADEMY SPECIAL

¼ cup shortening
1 cup sugar
1½ teaspoons vanilla
1 square chocolate, melted
1¼ cups flour, sifted
1¾ teaspoons baking powder
½ teaspoon salt

⅝ cup milk
¾ cup nut meats, toasted
1⅜ cups brown sugar
¼ cup cocoa
1¼ cups sugar
½ teaspoon salt
2¼ cups boiling water

Preheat oven to 350 degrees. Blend first 4 ingredients together. Add flour, baking powder and salt and blend together. Add milk and nut meats and beat well. Put into a greased and floured 8 x 11-inch pan. Mix together brown sugar, cocoa, sugar and salt. Spread over batter. Pour 2¼ cups boiling water over batter. Bake 1 hour. Makes a rich brownie with fudge sauce. May be made ahead and reheated for 5-7 minutes. Top with ice cream. Serves 12.

CHOCOLATE DECADENCE

1 pound dark sweet chocolate
10 tablespoons unsalted
  butter
4 whole eggs
1 tablespoon sugar

1 tablespoon flour
1 cup heavy cream, whipped
shaved bittersweet chocolate
1 10- to 12-ounce package
  frozen raspberries

Preheat oven to 425 degrees. Flour and butter an 8-inch round cake pan. Cut waxed paper to fit the bottom. Butter and lay it on the bottom of the pan. In a small saucepan over very low heat (or set into a larger saucepan of hot water), melt chocolate with butter. Set aside. In the deep top of a double boiler, combine eggs with sugar. Beat eggs and sugar over hot water until sugar dissolves and mixture is just lukewarm. Remove the top of double boiler from heat and beat eggs until they quadruple in volume and become quite thick. Fold flour into eggs. Stir ¼ of the egg mixture into the chocolate. Then, fold chocolate back into the rest of the egg mixture. Pour and scrape batter into cake pan. Bake 15 minutes. Cake will still be liquid in the center. Freeze cake overnight in the pan. To unmold cake, carefully dip the bottom of the pan in hot water. Invert it onto a cake plate. Remove pan and gently remove wax paper. Decorate cake with whipped cream and shaved chocolate. Refrigerate until serving. Puree raspberries and their juice in a blender or food processor. Strain out the seeds and serve a tablespoon of puree as a sauce with each portion. Very rich! A little goes a long way! Serves 12.

CREAM CHEESE POUND CAKE

1½ cups margarine
1 8-ounce package cream
  cheese
3 cups sugar

dash of salt
1½ teaspoons vanilla
6 large eggs
3 cups cake flour

Preheat oven to 325 degrees. Cream margarine, cream cheese and sugar. Add salt, vanilla and eggs, and mix well. Sift cake flour and add. Bake in a buttered and floured tube pan for 1½ hours. Cool in pan 10 minutes. Serves 6.

ONE-STEP POUND CAKE

2¼ cups flour
2 cups sugar
½ teaspoon salt
½ teaspoon soda
1 teaspoon grated lemon peel
1 teaspoon vanilla

1 cup butter or margarine,
  softened
1 8-ounce carton pineapple or
  mandarin orange yogurt
  (or 1 cup dairy sour
  cream)
3 eggs

Glaze:
1 cup powdered sugar

1-2 tablespoons lemon juice

Preheat oven to 325 degrees. Combine all ingredients in large mixer bowl and mix at low speed. Beat 3 minutes at medium speed. Pour into prepared pan and bake for 60 to 70 minutes until top of cake springs back when touched lightly in center. Cool cake upright in pan 15 minutes; remove from pan and cool completely. Combine powdered sugar and enough lemon juice to make drizzling consistency. Glaze cool cake.

ICING SUPREME

2¼ cups sugar
½ cup water
3 tablespoons white Karo syrup

3 egg whites
¼ cup powdered sugar

Mix sugar, water and Karo, and cook to 238 degrees on candy thermometer (or soft ball stage). Beat egg whites and pour hot syrup slowly over whites while beating. Add powdered sugar and beat until frosting loses its glaze. Yields enough for a 3 layer cake such as coconut or chocolate. Really good and easy!

MARGARITA'S FLAN

1 can condensed milk
1 can whole milk (measured
  in same can)

1 teaspoon vanilla
4 eggs
½ cup sugar

Preheat oven to 350 degrees. Mix first 4 ingredients in blender. Melt sugar to caramel in a small skillet on high heat. Cool slightly. Pour over other mixture, which has been placed in baine marie (pie pan in pan of water). Bake for 1 hour 15 minutes. Turn upside down on plate while warm.

PEANUT BUTTER ICE CREAM SQUARES

1¼ cups Graham cracker
crumbs
¼ cup sugar
6 tablespoons butter or
margarine, melted

1 cup dry roasted peanuts,
chopped
½ cup light corn syrup
⅓ cup chunky peanut butter
1 quart vanilla ice cream

Combine crumbs, sugar and butter. Press into bottom of a 9 x 9 x 2-inch baking pan. Place in freezer 30 minutes. Meanwhile, stir together ⅔ cup peanuts, corn syrup and peanut butter. Stir ice cream until it softens. Spoon half the softened ice cream evenly over chilled crust. Spread corn syrup mixture on top. Carefully spread remaining ice cream over all. Sprinkle with remaining ⅓ cup chopped peanuts. Cover and freeze until firm. Let stand at room temperature for 10 minutes before slicing. Serves 8.

CRANBERRY ICE

1 quart water
1 quart cranberries
(1 package)

3 cups sugar
juice of 2-3 lemons (or more
if desired)

Make syrup by boiling water and sugar together for 5 minutes. Set aside. Boil cranberries in a **little** water until soft, then press through sieve. Add syrup and lemon. Cool and freeze. Wonderful with Thanksgiving dinner!

ALICIA'S LEMON ICE

1 cup sugar
¾ cup freshly squeezed
lemon juice

finely grated rind of 3 lemons
1½ cups white corn syrup
4 cups milk

Combine sugar, lemon juice and rind. Beat with whisk to combine well. Add corn syrup and milk, whisking until smooth. Pour into a covered bowl, and place in freezer to freeze. Stir occasionally to ensure a smooth texture. Serves 8-10.

This is a lovely dinner party dessert when served with shortbread or a crisp refrigerator cookie.

A W NUTS

½ gallon vanilla ice cream
1 cup large pieces of pecans, toasted

1 cup coconut, toasted
¼ cup brandy or bourbon

Mix together and re-freeze. Easy and delicious!

ITALIAN CREAM CAKE

½ cup (4 tablespoons) butter or margarine
½ cup shortening
5 eggs, separated
2 cups sugar
1 cup buttermilk

2 cups flour, sifted
1 teaspoon baking soda
1 teaspoon vanilla
1 small can coconut
1 cup pecans, toasted and chopped

Frosting:
1 8-ounce package cream cheese
4 tablespoons butter or margarine, at room temperature

1 box powdered sugar, sifted
1 teaspoon vanilla
pecans, toasted and chopped

Preheat oven to 350 degrees. Soften margarine and shortening in microwave, and cream together in a large bowl. Fold in sugar and beat until smooth. Add egg yolks to mixture and beat well. Mix flour and soda; add to creamed mixture, alternating with buttermilk. Stir in vanilla, coconut and pecans. Beat egg whites and fold into mixture. Pour batter into 3 buttered and floured 9-inch cake pans. Bake for 25 minutes. Cool. Frosting: Soften cheese and margarine in microwave, and beat until smooth. Mix in sugar, add vanilla and beat. Spread between each layer of cake, then on top and on sides with a knife. Sprinkle top with toasted pecans. Serves 8.

ROMANO SAUCE (FOR BERRIES OR CAKE)

2 cups sour cream
½ cup brown sugar
2 tablespoons rum
2 tablespoons bourbon

¼ teaspoon cinnamon (optional)
1 pinch nutmeg (optional)

Mix well (a blender makes quick work of this) and allow to set for 1-2 hours in refrigerator. Yields 2½ cups.

Eggs and Cheese

Jefferson Historical Pilgrimage

For five decades the rich heritage of Jefferson has come alive each May as scenes from the past are reenacted.

Costumed artisans demonstrate early-day crafts. There is a regal Civil War presentation of the colors along with a Junior Historians' stage show. Performances of the infamous Diamond Bessie Murder Trial are featured along with art, music and the Pilgrimage Home Tour.

A bounty of fine food is served at the many historic restaurants and inns.

CHILIE EGG PUFF

8 ounces Monterey Jack
    cheese
5 eggs
1 cup cottage cheese
¼ cup butter or margarine,
    melted and cooled

¼ cup all purpose flour
½ teaspoon baking powder
¼ teaspoon salt
1 4-ounce can diced
    California green chilies

Insert shredding disc in food processor. Shred Jack cheese and set aside. Using metal blade of processor, process eggs 10 seconds. Add cottage cheese and butter and process another 10 seconds. Add flour, baking powder and salt and process with 2 on-and-off bursts. Add shredded cheese and chilies and process 1 second, or until just blended. Pour into an oiled 8-inch square pan. Bake 35 minutes at 350 degrees, or until edges brown and the center is firm. Serves 6-8.

CRUSTLESS QUICHE

¼ cup butter
5 eggs
¼ cup flour
½ teaspoon baking powder
⅛ teaspoon salt
½ pound large curd cottage
    cheese

½ pound Monterey Jack
    cheese, grated
2 cups of any special
    ingredients you like
    (examples below)

Melt butter. Whip the eggs until fluffy. Add flour, baking powder, salt, cottage cheese, melted butter and half the Monterey Jack cheese. Stir well. Add 2 cups of special ingredients. Place in an oiled 9-inch square pan and top with remaining Monterey Jack cheese. Bake at 400 degrees for 15 minutes, then reduce temperature to 350 degrees and continue to bake 30 to 35 more minutes, or until top is lightly browned. Possible ingredients: 6 ounces crab meat, drained; 10 sorrel leaves, cut into chiffonade (stack the leaves, roll them up and slice); or ¼ cup finely chopped parsley. Serves 4.

CRAB MEAT QUICHE

3 eggs, slightly beaten
1 cup sour cream
½ teaspoon Worcestershire
    sauce
¾ teaspoon salt
1 white onion, thinly sliced

3 tablespoons butter
½ pound Swiss cheese,
    coarsely grated
½ pound fresh white lump
    crab
1 unbaked 9-inch pastry shell

Preheat oven to 325 degrees. Combine eggs, sour cream, Worcestershire sauce and salt. In a large skillet, sauté onion in butter. Stir in cheese, crab and egg mixture. Pour into pre-baked pastry shell. Dot with butter. Bake 55 to 60 minutes, or until custard is set and knife inserted in center comes out clean. Serve hot. Serves 4-6.

Pastry shells can be pre-baked at 375 degrees for 10 minutes before filling is added to prevent soggy crust.

LOBSTER, CRAB OR CHICKEN QUICHE

1 unbaked 9-inch pastry shell
½ pound lobster, crab or
    chicken
⅓ cup mayonnaise
⅓ cup milk
2 eggs, beaten

1 tablespoon cornstarch
6 slices crumbled crisp bacon
2 cups chopped Cheddar
    cheese
⅓ cup sliced green onions
dash of pepper

Preheat oven to 350 degrees. Blend all ingredients together by hand. Turn into pre-baked pastry shell. Bake for 50 - 60 minutes. Serves 6-8.

SWISS EGGS IN A NEST

7 thin slices fresh bread
soft butter or margarine
Dijon mustard
1½ cups grated Swiss or mild
   Cheddar cheese
6 eggs

salt, pepper and curry powder
   to taste
¾ cup light or heavy cream
4 tablespoons grated
   Parmesan cheese

Preheat oven to 475 degrees. Remove crusts from bread and butter on both sides. Form a shell by fitting 6 slices, slightly overlapping with points up, in a 9-inch Corning or Pyrex pie plate, filling bottom with the last slice. Spread a little mustard on top part of each slice. Set in oven 5 to 6 minutes to toast slightly. Remove from oven and reduce heat to 350 degrees. Sprinkle shell with the Swiss or Cheddar cheese. Break eggs over cheese. Add salt and pepper, then sprinkle a bit of curry over. Pour cream over all, sprinkle with Parmesan and bake 10 to 13 minutes, or until eggs set. Good served with a green salad and toasted rolls. Serves 4-6.

CHICKEN FRITTATA

16 ounces egg substitute
¼ cup skim milk
2 tablespoons Dijon-style
   mustard
¼ teaspoon light salt
½ teaspoon pepper
2 cups chicken breast, cooked
   and chopped

1 10-ounce package frozen
   whole corn, thawed
1½ cups (about ½ pound)
   potatoes, cooked and
   cubed
¼ cup diced red pepper
2 tablespoons green onion,
   sliced

In a medium bowl, combine egg product, milk, mustard, salt and pepper. In a 12-inch, skillet sprayed with oil, cook remaining ingredients until vegetables are lightly browned, stirring occasionally. Stir in potatoes. Pour egg mixture over chicken-vegetable mixture. Cook over medium-low heat, 10 to 12 minutes or until egg product mixture is completely set. Serves 8.

PASTEL DE ELOTE
(A CORN, CHEESE AND GREEN CHILIE PIE)

4 large or 6 small ears of corn, enough to make 2 cups, or 2 packages frozen corn, thawed and drained
1 stick melted butter
2 eggs, beaten
½ cup yellow cornmeal
1½ teaspoons salt
1 cup sour cream
7 to 8 ounces diced Monterey Jack cheese
1 14-ounce can green chilies, peeled and diced

If using fresh corn, scrape the kernels from ears of corn, grating on a grater or using a corn scraper. If using frozen variety, drain corn (and rinse it if it was "frozen in butter sauce"). Put it into a blender container. Blend on low speed, forcing kernels into blades with a rubber spatula. Do not over-do this, as the mixture should not be smooth. Place corn in a large mixing bowl. Add melted butter, beaten eggs, cornmeal, salt, sour cream and diced cheese. Add chilies to cornmeal mixture. Pour into a well oiled, deep pie dish and bake at 350 degrees for 40 to 60 minutes, or until firm to the touch and golden brown. The flavor of this dish is vastly improved if the dish is chilled or frozen and then reheated to serve. This dish can and should be baked the day before serving, and reheated to serve. It is also quite delicious cold for lunch with a green salad. Freeze after baking. Makes a terrific side dish with charcoal broiled steaks. Serves 8.

WONDERFUL TOMATO TART

basic one crust pastry dough
8 ounces mozzarella cheese, shredded
2 tablespoons chopped fresh basil
4-5 ripe tomatoes, sliced ½-inch thick
½ teaspoon salt
¼ teaspoon freshly ground pepper
¼ cup virgin olive oil

Preheat oven to 400 degrees. Using a tart pan with removable bottom, line with pastry dough. Spread pastry with cheese and sprinkle with half the chopped basil. Cover cheese with sliced tomatoes and sprinkle with salt and pepper. Drizzle top with olive oil. Bake 30-40 minutes. Garnish with remaining basil. Slice in wedges and serve warm or at room temperature.

GATEAU FROMAGE

pastry for a 9-inch pie
½ pound sharp Cheddar
   cheese, grated
1 cup fresh onion rings
1 tablespoon oil
4 slices bacon

⅛ teaspoon pepper
¼ teaspoon salt
1 egg
1 tablespoon flour
¾ cup milk

Preheat oven to 450 degrees.

Line a 9-inch pie plate with pastry. Sprinkle with Cheddar cheese. Sauté onion rings in oil. Drain on paper toweling. Sauté bacon until crisp. Drain and crumble. Add onion rings and bacon to pie on top of cheese. Sprinkle with pepper and salt. Beat together the egg, flour and milk. Pour this mixture over cheese. Do not stir - jiggle the plate a little to combine. Bake in hot oven, 25 to 30 minutes, or until golden brown on top. Cool slightly before cutting. Serve warm. Green chilies, mushrooms, or other ingredients may be added. Serves 6-8.

AFTER CHRISTMAS QUICHE

2½ cups leftover cornbread
   dressing (or prepared
   chicken stuffing mix)
1 cup chopped, cooked turkey
1 cup shredded Swiss cheese
4 eggs, beaten

1 5⅓-ounce can evaporated
   milk
⅛ teaspoon white pepper
tomato wedges (optional)
paprika (optional)

Preheat oven to 350 degrees. Press leftover dressing into a 9-inch pie plate, forming a crust. Bake 10 minutes at 400 degrees. Combine meat and cheese. In another container, combine eggs, milk and pepper. Sprinkle meat and cheese mixture into hot crust. Pour egg and milk mixture on top. Bake 30 to 35 minutes at 350 degrees, or until center is set. Cool at least 10 minutes before serving. Garnish with tomato wedges and paprika, if desired. Serves 6.

ORANGE FRENCH TOAST

4 eggs (or 3 extra-large)
⅔ cup orange juice
⅓ cup milk or half and half
¼ cup sugar
¼ teaspoon nutmeg
½ teaspoon vanilla

1 8-ounce baguette (loaf of French bread), cut into 1-inch slices
⅓ cup melted butter
½ cup pecan pieces
powdered sugar for garnish
orange slices for garnish

With a wire whisk, beat together eggs, orange juice, milk, sugar, nutmeg and vanilla. Place bread in a single layer to fit tightly in a 9 x 13-inch casserole. Pour mixture over bread. Let it set a few minutes, then turn to coat other side well. Cover and refrigerate overnight. If you can, turn bread once, several hours later. Preheat oven to 400 degrees. Pour melted butter into a different 9 x 13-inch baking dish. Spread butter evenly (put a bit around the sides of the dish also). Arrange soaked bread slices in a single layer in the dish. Sprinkle with pecan pieces. Bake until golden brown, about 20 to 25 minutes. When removed from the oven, sprinkle with a hint of powdered sugar for presentation. Garnish with orange slices. To prepare a low-fat recipe, use egg substitute, skim or 1 per cent milk and low-fat margarine. Serves 4.

PUFFED GERMAN APPLE PANCAKE

6 eggs
1 cup milk
⅔ cups flour
½ teaspoon salt
4 tablespoons butter
3 medium apples, peeled, cored, and sliced

¼ cup fresh lemon juice (divided use)
¼ cup firmly packed dark brown sugar
½ teaspoon cinnamon

Preheat oven to 425 degrees. Mix together eggs, milk, flour and salt. Toss apple slices with 2 tablespoons lemon juice. In a 13 x 9-inch baking dish or 12-inch fluted porcelain quiche dish, melt butter in preheated oven. Remove dish from oven, and place apple slices evenly over bottom of dish and return to oven until butter sizzles. Do not allow to brown. Remove from oven and immediately pour batter over apples. Mix together brown sugar and cinnamon; sprinkle over batter. Return to oven and bake 20 minutes or until puffed and brown. Drizzle 2 tablespoons lemon juice on top. Yields 8-10 servings.

PASHKA WITH APPLE WEDGES

4 8-ounce packages cream
   cheese, softened
½ pound sweet butter
2 cups powdered sugar

2 teaspoons vanilla
finely grated rind of 1 lemon
1 cup sliced almonds, toasted
fresh fruit for garnish

Cream together cream cheese and butter. Add powdered sugar, vanilla and lemon rind. Mix until smooth and fold in almonds. Pour mixture into a damp cheese cloth that has been placed in a mold with a hole in the center. Place over a dish or plate. Refrigerate overnight. Turn out of mold and garnish with fresh fruit, such as apple wedges. To prevent apples from turning dark, wash wedges in orange juice. Drain well when ready to serve. Serves 6-8.

HOPPEL POPPEL

2½ cups kosher salami,
   cooked and chopped or
   cubed
6 green onions, finely
   chopped

2 tomatoes, peeled and diced
½ cup green pepper, diced
¼ teaspoon pepper
12 eggs, slightly beaten

Preheat oven to 350 degrees. Mix ingredients thoroughly. Pour into shallow buttered 9 x 13-inch pan. Bake for about 10 to 12 minutes, or until set.

BREAKFAST PIZZA

1 pound pork sausage
1 package crescent rolls
1 cup frozen hash browns
1 cup shredded Cheddar
   cheese

2 tablespoons Parmesan
   cheese
5 eggs, beaten
¼ cup milk
½ teaspoon salt
⅛ teaspoon pepper

Brown sausage and drain. Spread dough on pizza pan, making a tall lip. Sprinkle with the sausage, then hash browns, then top with cheese. Pour the mixture of eggs, milk, salt and pepper on top. Bake at 350 degrees for 30 to 35 minutes, or until browned. Yields 8 servings.

Meats

Gladewater East Texas Gusher Days

Gladewater rekindles the nostalgia of the "oil boom days" each April. The GUSHER of events includes a 1930's musical comedy, Pioneer Luncheon, fishing, golf and horseshoe tournaments, antique car show, street dance, carnival and a 5K Gusher Gallop.

Capping off the festivities is the annual Gusher Days Chili Cook-Off. Cooks come from Texas and Louisiana to prepare their award-winning chili. Along with demonstrations of their culinary skills, they also take part in a showmanship competition. Just like the chili, things can get a little bit hot!

A trip to Kilgore to the East Texas Oil Museum which depicts the colorful wildcatting days of early oil discoveries is a must!

MAGIC TENDERLOIN

1 tenderloin, any size   garlic powder
fresh cracked pepper

Very Important: Let tenderloin come to room temperature. Cover entire outer surface with fresh cracked pepper and a light coating of garlic powder. Preheat oven to 400 degrees. Place uncovered tenderloin on a rack in a pan. Place in the oven. Cook 6 minutes per pound. Turn the oven off. Leave the meat in the hot oven for 2 hours, or until time to eat, whichever is longer. DON'T PEEK! Will be well done on the outside and pink on the inside. Salt may be added before serving, if desired.

BEEF TENDER WITH MUSTARD-HORSERADISH CREAM

1 beef tenderloin, 5 to 7   ½ cup liquid smoke
   pounds, trimmed   cracked pepper
3 tablespoons olive oil   ¼ cup melted margarine
1 tablespoon garlic powder   (optional)
1 tablespoon seasoned salt

Mustard-Horseradish Cream:
1 cup whipping cream   ¼ cup bottled white
¼ cup Dijon mustard   horseradish
                                          juice of 1 lemon

To make mustard cream, whip 1 cup cream until stiff. Fold in ¼ cup mustard, ¼ cup bottled horseradish and the juice of 1 lemon. Refrigerate until serving time. Rub the beef with oil and liquid smoke. Then rub in garlic powder and seasoned salt. Finish with a grind of pepper. Cover and refrigerate for at least 12 hours. To cook, preheat oven to 375 degrees. Remove beef from marinade and place in roasting pan. If desired, pour melted margarine over tender. Roast uncovered for 40 minutes, or until a meat thermometer inserted at thickest point registers 140 degrees. Turn the meat once while cooking. Remove from oven and allow to stand about 10 minutes. Cut into slices. Serve with Mustard-Horseradish Cream. Makes 8-10 servings. Note: If you have a smaller tender, cut the cooking time accordingly. For example, 25 minutes for 4 pounds.

GARLIC STEAKS

4 cloves garlic, minced
½ cup fresh Parmesan cheese
3 tablespoons butter,
    softened
2 tablespoons Marsala wine

1 tablespoon brandy
1 teaspoon tomato paste
½ teaspoon black pepper
4 filet mignons

Combine all ingredients except meat in a food processor. Blend to a paste consistency. Grill steaks to desired degree of doneness. Spread paste evenly over steaks and continue cooking until mixture begins to bubble, about 1 to 2 minutes longer.

BARBECUED BRISKET

1 freshly cut center beef
    brisket, about 6 pounds
1 large onion, sliced
1 clove garlic, halved

12 whole cloves
12 peppercorns
1 bay leaf

Sauce:
3 cups catsup
⅓ cup Worcestershire sauce
3 tablespoons firmly packed
    light brown sugar

2 tablespoons dry mustard
    (yes, tablespoons!)
1 cup water

Place brisket in a large pot. Cover with water. Add onion, garlic, cloves, peppercorns and bay leaf. Bring slowly to a boil; reduce heat. Cover and simmer 3 to 3½ hours or until meat is firm-tender, not falling apart. Remove pot from heat. Let meat cool in liquid. (This is important - keeps meat from being dry and stringy.) Remove meat. Trim off any remaining fat. Slice cooked meat across the grain. Preheat oven to 350 degrees. In a medium bowl mix catsup, Worcestershire sauce, sugar, mustard and water. Spoon ½ cup of the sauce over sliced meat. Reserve remainder. Bake, covered, 45 minutes or until meat is tender and heated through, brushing with the reserved sauce in the baking dish. Heat remaining sauce and serve with the brisket. This may be frozen before the last baking step.

VENISON STEW IN CROCK POT

2 pounds venison back strap,
    sliced 1 inch (or more)
    thick
3 ribs celery, cut diagonally
    into 1-inch pieces
½ cup green onions (save
    tops for adding later)
2 cloves garlic, minced
1 tablespoon parsley,
    chopped

¼ teaspoon oregano
½ cup water
½ cup dry red wine
1 8-ounce can tomato sauce,
    unsalted
2 tablespoons olive oil
potatoes and carrots,
    chopped

Season meat with seasoned pepper, lemon herb seasoning, unsalted meat tenderizer or your own seasoning. Brown meat lightly in oil in a hot skillet. Place celery and onions in bottom of crock pot. Add browned meat slices and remaining ingredients. Cover and cook on high for 3 hours, stirring occasionally. Add potatoes, carrots and onion tops. Cook on low until vegetables are done. Serves 8.

MARINATED PORK TENDERLOIN

¼ cup bourbon
¼ cup soy sauce
¼ cup brown sugar, packed
3 cloves garlic, minced
1 teaspoon fresh ginger,
    minced (or ¼ teaspoon
    powdered ginger)

1 teaspoon Worcestershire
    sauce
¼ cup vegetable oil
2 1-pound pork tenderloins

Combine all ingredients, except pork, with a whisk or in food processor. Place tenderloin and marinade in a ziploc bag in the refrigerator overnight. Broil 6 inches from heat for 16-18 minutes. Baste often. Slice in ½-inch thick slices to serve as a main course, or slice in ¼-inch slices to put on top of French bread for a picnic. Serves 6.

BUTTERFLIED LEG OF LAMB

6 to 7 pounds leg of lamb,
   butterflied
1 clove garlic, crushed
2 teaspoons salt
½ teaspoon basil
½ teaspoon garlic salt
1 bay leaf

¾ cup olive oil
¼ cup red wine vinegar
½ cup green onion, chopped
2 teaspoons Dijon mustard
½ teaspoon oregano
¼ teaspoon black pepper

Place the butterflied lamb, fat side down, in a shallow baking dish. Combine the remaining ingredients and pour over the lamb. Cover and marinate 12 hours in the refrigerator, turning once. Remove from refrigerator 1 hour before cooking. Broil 4 inches from heat in oven for ten minutes. Turn, baste, and broil another 10 minutes. Then bake 10-15 minutes at 425 degrees. Carve into thin slices. Serves 8.

PERFECT ROAST LEG OF LAMB

1 6-pound leg of lamb, fat
   removed
2 garlic cloves, minced
1 tablespoon paprika

1 tablespoon dried rosemary
2 teaspoons salt
½ teaspoon pepper

Orange Basting Sauce:
½ cup butter
1 6-ounce can frozen orange
   juice concentrate,
   thawed and undiluted

¼ cup dry red wine

Preheat oven to 350 degrees. Make 12 slits in lamb with paring knife. Combine seasonings and press a little into each slit. Insert a meat thermometer into thickest part of lamb, being careful to not touch bone. Put into oven and roast to desired doneness using scale below. Mix basting sauce and frequently baste lamb after 1 hour of cooking. Continue to baste until done. Let set 15 minutes and carve to serve. Roasting Scale: Roast 12 to 15 minutes per pound (130 - 135 degrees on thermometer) for rare, 20 minutes per pound (140 degrees) for medium or 30-35 minutes per pound (160 degrees) for well-done. Serves 6-8.

QUESADILLAS WITH BEEF

1 teaspoon salt
1 pound lean ground beef
½ cup onion, finely chopped
1 clove garlic, minced
½ teaspoon oregano,
    crumbled

1 8-ounce can tomato sauce
1 dozen 8-inch flour tortillas
¾ pound Cheddar or
    Monterey Jack cheese (or
    mixture), shredded
¼ pound butter or margarine

Sprinkle salt into large frying pan. Add ground beef and onion. Sauté over high heat, stirring until crumbly. Add garlic, oregano and tomato sauce. Simmer uncovered until liquid evaporates. Sprinkle one tortilla with about ½ cup cheese and spoon over about ⅓ cup of meat mixture. Cover with a second tortilla. Melt 2 tablespoons butter in a large frying pan over medium high heat. Lay in the filled tortillas and cook until golden underneath. Turn over carefully with a wide spatula and brown other side. If you make all ahead, place in a baking pan, uncovered, and keep warm in a 250 degree oven. Continue to fill and cook the remaining tortillas in the same manner. Serves 6.

THE REAL MCCOY STEAK

2 pounds top sirloin,
    cut 2½ inches thick
2 tablespoons bleu or
    Roquefort cheese
1 large clove garlic, chopped
    fine
1 teaspoon coarse black
    pepper

1 teaspoon salt
1 tablespoon soy sauce
1 heaping tablespoon
    powdered instant coffee
1 tablespoon Worcestershire
    sauce
¼ cup cooking oil

To prepare marinade, mix cheese, garlic, pepper, salt, soy sauce, coffee, Worcestershire sauce and oil in food processor. Pour over steak and rub into meat; save excess to baste steak while it is cooking. Marinate in refrigerator 2 hours, or overnight if desired. Place steak on the rack in broiler pan 4 to 5 inches from heat. Broil for 25 minutes for medium rare (150 degrees), turning once. Carve steak across grain into thin slices. Serves 8.

BEER BEEF STEW

2 small yellow onions, sliced
1 clove garlic, crushed
½ stick margarine or butter,
   divided
1 pound cubed lean chuck or
   stew meat
¼ teaspoon thyme
¼ teaspoon sage

1 bay leaf
2 cups beef broth
¼ cup strong beer
1 tablespoon butter
1 tablespoon flour
2 pounds small red new
   potatoes

Mix the 1 tablespoon butter and 1 tablespoon flour together. Set aside. Peel potatoes and roast in oven until done (may be par-boiled, brushed with butter and then roasted in a 375 degree oven for 30 to 45 minutes). Sauté garlic and onion in 2 tablespoons butter until soft. Add 2 more tablespoons butter and brown meat. Add all remaining ingredients except for flour/butter mixture and the potatoes. Simmer about 1 hour. Add flour and butter that has been mixed together a little at a time until the sauce is thickened. Serve over new potatoes. Garnish with parsley. Delicious with Irish brown bread and salad. Serves 4.

BEEF AND BROCCOLI

2 tablespoons soy sauce
1 or 2 teaspoons cornstarch
1 tablespoon Hoi Sin sauce
1 tablespoon oyster flavored
   sauce
1 tablespoon Mirin (rice
   cooking vinegar)

sirloin steak
sesame oil
garlic
ginger
broccoli, fresh, cut in small
   florets

Mix soy sauce and cornstarch. Add Hoi Sin sauce, oyster flavored sauce and Mirin. Set sauce aside. Cut sirloin in narrow strips. Sauté or stir-fry in cooking oil with a few drops of sesame oil, garlic and ginger, until redness is gone. Remove. Stir-fry broccoli 1 minute. Put beef and sauce back in wok with broccoli and cook for 1 to 2 minutes. Serve over rice.

TALLERINE

1 12-ounce package egg
  noodles
2 pounds chili-grind ground
  beef
2 large onions, chopped
½ bell pepper, chopped
2 cloves garlic, chopped

2 teaspoons chili powder
salt and pepper to taste
1 can whole kernel corn
1 can tomato soup
1 can Rotel tomatoes
3 cups Cheddar or Monterey
  Jack cheese, grated

Brown beef. Add onions and bell pepper. Cook until tender. Add garlic, chili powder, salt and pepper. While beef cooks, boil noodles until tender. Drain. Put half of the cooked noodles in bottom of a large casserole. Spread meat mixture over noodles, then corn, then a layer of cheese (saving some for top of casserole). Spread remaining noodles on top. Pour tomato soup diluted with half a can of water and the can of tomatoes over the casserole. Cook 1 to 1½ hours at 250 to 300 degrees. Just before serving, sprinkle with remaining cheese. Serves 8-10.

AWARD WINNING CHILI

2 pounds ground beef
1 tablespoon cumin
⅓ cup chili powder
½ to 1 teaspoon cayenne
  pepper
½ teaspoon paprika

1 teaspoon salt
2 tablespoons dried onions
1 8-ounce can tomato sauce
1 28-ounce can chopped
  tomatoes
1 cup water

Brown meat. Drain well. Add seasonings and tomato sauce. Add tomatoes and water. Cover and simmer 1½ hours, stirring occasionally. Serve topped with grated Cheddar cheese and sour cream over rice, if desired. Serves 6-8.

BEEF MADEIRA

4 tablespoons butter, divided
2½ pounds beef tenderloin
1 teaspoon salt
¼ teaspoon pepper
4 large mushrooms, sliced

3 tablespoons finely chopped
   shallots
½ cup Madeira (or any red
   wine)
1 10¾-ounce can beef gravy

Melt 2 tablespoons butter in shallow roasting pan in oven while preheating oven to 425 degrees. Turn beef in butter to coat evenly. Sprinkle with salt and pepper. Roast beef 45 to 50 minutes. Meanwhile, sauté mushrooms in skillet over medium high heat in remaining 2 tablespoons butter until mushrooms give up their juice. Add shallots. Cook 3 minutes while stirring. Add wine and cook for 1 minute. Stir in gravy. Reduce heat and simmer 15 minutes. Remove roast to carving board and keep warm. Pour off fat and pour wine sauce into roasting pan. Stir and scrape sides with wooden spoon. Slice meat and serve with gravy drizzled on top. Serves 4-6.

MAMA'S MEXICAN DINNER

1 pound ground meat
1 onion, chopped
2 3-ounce cans chopped
   green chilies
1 10-ounce can or jar taco
   sauce
1 8-ounce can tomato sauce
1 tablespoon chili powder

1 10-ounce can enchilada
   sauce
2 cans mushroom soup
12 corn tortillas
¾ pound Monterey Jack
   cheese, grated
¾ pound Cheddar cheese,
   grated

Brown meat. Drain well and add onion, chilies, sauces, soup and chili powder. Spray a large glass casserole with vegetable oil spray, and line with 6 tortillas. Pour ½ the meat mixture on top. Top with the Monterey Jack cheese. Layer with the remaining tortillas, then the meat mixture, and top with the grated Cheddar cheese. Bake at 350 degrees for 35 to 40 minutes until the cheese melts and bubbles. Serves 10-12.

HAM AND SPINACH ROLLS

24 thin slices boiled ham
2 10-ounce packages frozen
   chopped spinach
2 cups packaged cornbread
   stuffing
2 cups sour cream
8 tablespoons butter

8 tablespoons flour
1 cup milk
½ cup sharp Cheddar cheese,
   grated
paprika
Parmesan cheese

Cook spinach and drain well. Combine spinach, cornbread stuffing and sour cream. Spread on ham slices. Roll ham slices and put in baking pan "seam side" down. Make cheese sauce with butter, flour, milk and Cheddar cheese. Pour over ham rolls. Sprinkle with paprika and Parmesan cheese. Bake at 350 degrees for 15 minutes covered and 15 minutes uncovered. Serves 8-12.

FAJITAS FROM THE RAW DEAL, AUSTIN, TEXAS

½ cup Italian dressing
½ cup soy sauce
½ cup apple cider vinegar
⅓ cup Worcestershire sauce
⅓ cup brown sugar, packed

1 teaspoon garlic powder
juice of 1 lime
2 pounds skirt steak
flour tortillas

Make marinade by combining all ingredients except skirt steak and tortillas. Cut as much fat from the meat as possible, and cut into 5- to 6-ounce portions. Cover with marinade. Marinate meat 24 hours in refrigerator. Drain and grill. Slice thinly across the grain and pile into flour tortillas. Add fresh salsa, sour cream, guacamole and black beans, as desired. Serves 6.

Pasta

Jacksonville Tomato Fest

In September, Jacksonville celebrates the star of their summer season with the annual Tomato Fest.

The "couch potato" gives way to the "couch tomato" during the weekend's festivities. History takes on new meaning as participants engage in the Battle of San Tomato!

The Red Hot Tomato Bike Tour brings riders from throughout the state. There are also horseshoe and washer tournaments, entertainment, handcrafts and much more.

Of course, on hand in bushels and pecks is the red, redoubtable star, Mr. Top Tomato!

ARTICHOKE AND SHRIMP SAUCE

⅓ cup bacon, chopped
¼ cup onion, chopped
2 tablespoons butter or
  margarine
1 cup heavy cream
1 9-ounce package frozen
  artichoke hearts, thawed
  and quartered
½ cup canned tomatoes,
  undrained and chopped

1 teaspoon dried marjoram,
  crumbled
½ teaspoon salt
⅛ teaspoon black pepper
¼ teaspoon ground nutmeg
4 ounces cooked small shrimp
hot cooked pasta
grated Parmesan cheese

In saucepan, sauté bacon and onion in butter or margarine over medium heat until bacon is barely crisp. Stir in all remaining ingredients except shrimp, pasta and Parmesan cheese. Simmer uncovered until artichokes are tender and sauce is thickened. At this point, sauce may be stored in refrigerator as long as 6 to 8 hours. Before serving, stir shrimp into the artichoke mixture. Heat until hot. Serve sauce over hot pasta, and top with Parmesan cheese.

BURGUNDY POPPY SEED PASTA

1 package bow-tie pasta
  (spinach is pretty)
2 cups Granny Smith apples,
  unpeeled and finely
  chopped
½ large package frozen green
  peas, thawed

½ cup pecans, toasted and
  chopped
2 small cans mandarin
  orange slices
fresh spinach leaves
½ bottle Burgundy Poppy
  Seed Salad Dressing

Cook pasta according to package directions. Drain and allow to cool. Mix with other ingredients and serve on a bed of spinach leaves. Serves 8.

MEATBALLS AND SPAGHETTI

Meatballs:
1 large onion, grated
olive oil (to cook onion)
1 pound ground beef
1 pound ground pork (have
   meat market run
   combined beef and pork
   through grinder twice)
2 eggs, beaten

1 cup grated Parmesan
   cheese
1 cup bread crumbs
¾ cup milk
½ cup flour
2 or 3 garlic cloves, minced
dash red pepper
salt and pepper to taste
1 teaspoon oregano

Tomato Sauce:
1 onion, chopped
3 14½-ounce cans tomatoes
2 6-ounce cans tomato paste
1 8-ounce can tomato sauce
1 cup water
1 tablespoon sugar

2 or 3 garlic cloves, minced
1 bay leaf
1 teaspoon oregano
dash red pepper
salt and pepper to taste

Meatballs: Sauté onion in olive oil until translucent, and set aside. Mix beef, pork, eggs, Parmesan cheese, bread crumbs, milk, flour, garlic, spices and cooked onion. Mix well. Shape into 2½-inch balls and brown in skillet (in olive oil) on all sides. (Variation: broil under broiler until brown on all sides.) Add browned meatballs to tomato sauce and simmer 30 minutes. Tomato Sauce: In olive oil, brown onion in large (8-quart) pot. Add remaining ingredients and simmer at least 30 minutes. Double all recipes to serve 12. Recipe serves 6.

Tomato Tips: In Jacksonville and all over East Texas, a tomato plucked from the vine, eaten on the spot with the warmth of the midday sun, is said to be the best way to savor its flavor.
- *Don't refrigerate tomatoes — ever!*
- *To stuff tomatoes, make a shell by cutting a slice off the top and hollowing out with a small spoon, or cut the tomato crosswise in half and hollow each half. Turn them upside down on a paper towel to drain before stuffing.*
- *To ripen tomatoes, put in a closed paper bag, not on a sunny windowsill.*

MOTHER'S LASAGNA

2 tablespoons olive oil
1 pound ground beef round
5 cups basic tomato sauce
4 tablespoons chopped fresh
parsley, divided use
3½ cups ricotta cheese
1 cup chopped cooked
spinach, well drained

¼ cup freshly grated
Parmesan cheese
1 tablespoon dried oregano
¾ teaspoon ground nutmeg
fresh ground pepper to taste
8 lasagna noodles, cooked al
dente
3 cups grated mozzarella
cheese

Preheat oven to 350 degrees. Heat olive oil in a skillet over medium heat. Add beef and cook, stirring occasionally, until browned. Drain and set aside. Place tomato sauce in a saucepan. Add beef and 2 tablespoons parsley, and cook over medium heat for 3 minutes. Remove pan from heat. In a mixing bowl, combine ricotta cheese, spinach, Parmesan, remaining 2 tablespoons parsley, oregano, nutmeg and pepper. Stir well. Place 2 cups of tomato sauce in the bottom of a 13 x 9-inch baking dish. Arrange 4 noodles on top of the sauce. Spread half the ricotta mixture over lasagna, and sprinkle with 1 cup mozzarella. Repeat the layers of sauce, noodles, ricotta and mozzarella. Top with remaining 2 cups of sauce and 1 cup mozzarella sprinkled evenly on top. Cover dish loosely with aluminum foil and place on baking sheet, and bake for 45 minutes. Remove foil and bake an additional 20 minutes. Serves 8.

*All over East Texas in the last decade we have seen the age of pasta arrive. It is loved for its health benefits as well as its versatility. **"When is it done?"** is an often-asked question. First of all, pasta must be tasted to know when it is cooked. Fish out a strand and bite it after about four minutes of cooking for dried pasta. It should be firm yet tender. **Al dente**, so often used to describe perfectly-cooked pasta, translates as "to the tooth", meaning it should have some firmness remaining — not too hard or too soft — but just right! Cook another minute or two if too firm — but not until soft as this spoils its texture.*

LINGUINE WITH TOMATO BASIL SAUCE

1 medium onion, chopped
1 small clove garlic, minced
2 tablespoons olive oil
1 14-ounce can Italian style
  tomatoes, undrained and
  chopped
1 tablespoon dried basil (or ⅓
  cup fresh)
¾ teaspoon sugar
¼ teaspoon dried whole
  oregano (or ¾ teaspoon
  fresh)
¼ teaspoon salt
⅛ teaspoon pepper
¼ cup milk
8 ounces uncooked linguine
¼ cup grated Parmesan
  cheese

Sauté onion and garlic in olive oil in a large skillet over medium heat. Add next 6 ingredients. Bring mixture to a boil; continue to boil 5 minutes or until most of the liquid evaporates. Reduce heat. Stir in milk and simmer 5 minutes. Set aside. Cook linguine according to package directions, omitting salt. Drain well. Pour tomato sauce over hot linguine, and toss well. Sprinkle with Parmesan cheese. Note: For a heartier meal, add spicy Italian sausage or 1 pound browned ground meat. On a somewhat healthier note, try boiled shrimp, crawfish, clams, mussels, scallops, or a combination. Serves 4-6.

CHICKEN TETRAZZINI

1 8-ounce package spaghetti
1¾ cups grated Cheddar
  cheese, divided
4 tablespoons Parmesan
  cheese, divided
4 cups cooked chicken or
  turkey, divided
1 2-ounce can diced pimentos
1 green pepper, cut in thin
  slices
1 small yellow onion, minced
1 10½-ounce can cream of
  mushroom soup
1 cup chicken broth
¼ cup dry white wine
  (optional)
salt and pepper to taste

Cook and drain spaghetti. Combine 1¼ cups Cheddar cheese, 2 tablespoons Parmesan cheese and all remaining ingredients. Toss with the spaghetti. Place in oiled casserole dish and sprinkle with reserved cheeses. Cook, covered, for 45 minutes at 350 degrees. May be frozen, or made ahead and reheated. Serves 6-8.

CHICKEN PASTA PRIMAVERA

1 large white or yellow onion, chopped
2 cloves garlic, crushed
8 ounces fresh mushrooms, sliced
4 large skinless chicken breast halves, cubed
2 large yellow squash, julienned
2 carrots, julienned (optional)
2 medium zucchini, julienned
1 box fresh mushrooms, sliced
8 ounces heavy cream
1 8-ounce package fideo pasta
freshly grated Romano cheese

Sauté onion and garlic in 2 tablespoons margarine until translucent. Add mushrooms and sauté until tender. Remove from skillet and set aside. Sauté chicken in 2 tablespoons margarine (more if needed) over medium to medium-high heat just until done. Return onion mixture to skillet with chicken. Add squash, carrots, zucchini. Sauté until tender. Add heavy cream and heat thoroughly over low to medium-low heat. Do not boil. While mixture is simmering, prepare noodles according to package directions. Drain noodles and toss with olive oil or margarine to prevent noodles from sticking together. Serve chicken mixture over hot noodles and sprinkle with Romano cheese. Serve with salad and hot French bread. Serves 6.

NOODLES ROMANOFF

hot cooked noodles (5 to 6 ounces uncooked)
1 cup cottage cheese
1 to 1½ cups sour cream
¼ cup finely chopped green onion
1 clove garlic, minced
1 teaspoon Worcestershire sauce
dash of Tabasco
¼ teaspoon salt (optional)
½ cup grated sharp cheese

Heat oven to 350 degrees. Mix all ingredients, except sharp cheese, and place in oiled 8 x 8 x 2-inch square baking dish. Sprinkle with cheese. Bake 40 minutes. May easily be doubled for large numbers. This recipe serves 4-6.

WIDE PASTA WITH GRILLED TOMATOES

4 large ripe tomatoes, cored
   and sliced crosswise, ⅓-
   inch thick
2 tablespoons minced garlic
3 tablespoons olive oil,
   divided
1 teaspoon red wine vinegar

¼ cup chopped fresh basil
salt and fresh ground pepper
12 strips (10 ounces) dried
   lasagna, cut into 1 x 3-
   inch pieces after cooked
grated Parmesan cheese
whole basil leaves

Place tomato slices on large heavy baking sheet and broil until browned. Turn once. Transfer to large bowl. Cook garlic in a skillet in 1 tablespoon olive oil over low heat for 5 minutes, stirring frequently. Add to tomatoes with 1 tablespoon olive oil, vinegar and basil. Stir gently and add salt and pepper to taste. Boil lasagna until al dente, about 5 to 6 minutes. Add 2 table-spoons lasagna "cooking water" to tomato mixture, then drain pasta. Stir 1 tablespoon olive oil into lasagna, then add to toma-toes. Place on 4 plates, add cheese, garnish with whole basil leaves and serve. Serves 4.

FETTUCINE ALFREDO

12 ounces fresh or 8 ounces
   dried fettucine
2 tablespoons butter or
   margarine
¾ cup heavy cream or half
   and half

½ cup grated Parmesan
   cheese, divided use
freshly grated nutmeg
salt and freshly ground
   pepper

While pasta is cooking, melt butter in a large skillet. Add cream and ¼ cup cheese. Simmer over very low heat 4 to 5 minutes until sauce starts to thicken, stirring constantly. Drain pasta well and add to skillet. Stir to combine all ingredients and to coat pasta with sauce. Add remaining cheese, nutmeg, salt and a generous grinding of black pepper. Serve on warm plates. Variation: Add ¼ teaspoon red pepper flakes to skillet when butter has melted. Serves 3-4.

FETTUCINE WITH GORGONZOLA
AND FRESH CORN SAUCE

6 tablespoons minced red onion
¼ cup olive oil
¼ teaspoon salt
1½ cups evaporated low fat milk
6 ounces Gorgonzola, crumbled
Tabasco, several dashes
1 pound fettucine

1½ teaspoons grated lemon rind
12 large basil leaves cut into thin strips
6 large mint leaves cut into thin strips
1½ cups fresh corn, scraped from the ear
8 thick slices bacon, fried very crisp and crumbled
whole basil leaves

In a medium skillet, wilt onions in olive oil without browning. Add salt and milk, stir, then add cheese and Tabasco and stir. Cook over low heat, stirring until cheese is melted and thickened. Remove from heat. Cook pasta according to package directions and drain. When fettucine is almost done, reheat sauce, adding all remaining ingredients except bacon. Cook 1 minute, stirring. Toss pasta with ½ the sauce. Top each serving with 2 tablespoons sauce and sprinkle with bacon for garnish. Also use a few whole basil leaves to garnish.

- *Use **Red Sauce for Pasta** or **Fresh Tomato Sauce** found in the Sauces section over any cooked pasta of your choice.*
- *To peel tomatoes, drop into a pot of boiling water for 1 to 2 minutes, depending on size. Scoop out and drop into ice water. Remove the stem and skin should slip off.*

SPINACH PESTO WITH PASTA

Pesto:
3 cups loosely packed fresh
   spinach leaves
2 cups fresh parsley
½ cup grated Parmesan
   cheese
½ cup grated Romano cheese
½ cup olive oil

¼ cup blanched almonds
¼ cup (½ stick) butter,
   melted
2 tablespoons pine nuts,
   toasted
3 large garlic cloves, crushed
¼ teaspoon salt

Pasta:
1 tablespoon oil
½ teaspoons salt

1 pound pasta, cooked

For pesto, puree first 10 ingredients in blender, or food processor until smooth, and set aside. For pasta, bring water to boil in large pan. Add oil and salt. Add pasta and cook over medium-high heat until al dente. Strain through colander, reserving ¼ cup liquid. Blend hot liquid into puree and toss with pasta. Serve with Parmesan cheese. May be frozen, or prepared ahead and re-heated. Serves 4.

LINGUINE WITH CLAM SAUCE

1 16-ounce package linguine
2 cloves garlic, minced
½ cup butter or margarine,
   melted
2 6½-ounce cans minced
   clams, drained
½ teaspoon dried whole basil
   (or 1½ teaspoons fresh,
   chopped)

½ teaspoon dried whole
   oregano (or 1½
   teaspoons fresh,
   chopped)
¼ teaspoon salt
¼ teaspoon pepper
½ cup chopped fresh parsley
1 cup grated Parmesan
   cheese

Cook linguine according to package directions. Drain and return to pan and set aside. Sauté garlic in butter in a medium skillet; add clams and next 4 ingredients. Cook over low heat, stirring constantly for 5 minutes. Pour over hot cooked linguine. Add parsley and toss gently. Place on a warm platter and top with freshly grated Parmesan cheese. Serves 4-6.

BASIC PIZZA DOUGH RECIPE

1 teaspoon salt
1 tablespoon honey
2 tablespoons olive oil
¾ cup cool water
1 envelope active dry yeast
¼ cup warm water

3 cups all purpose flour
(or 1½ cups whole wheat
flour and 1½ cups all
purpose flour)
a pizza stone

Preheat oven to 450 or 475 degrees. In a small mixing bowl, combine salt, honey, olive oil and cool water. Mix well. In a separate bowl, sprinkle yeast over warm water and let proof for 10 minutes. Place flour in bowl of food processor. With motor running, slowly pour honey mixture through feed tube; then pour in yeast. Process until dough forms a ball around blade. Transfer dough to a lightly floured surface and knead until smooth. Place in buttered bowl and allow dough to rest, covered, for 30 minutes. Divide dough into 4 equal parts. Form each piece into a smooth ball, flatten slightly and place on a plate. Cover each plate with a damp towel and refrigerate. One hour before baking, let dough come to room temperature. Lightly flour work surface. Flatten each ball of dough into a 7-inch circle. Pat out. Garnish as desired. Bake on a pizza stone for 10 to 12 minutes, or until golden. May be frozen. Yields 4.

BLACK FOREST HAM AND GOAT CHEESE PIZZA

¼ cup plus 2 tablespoons
    olive oil
2 small eggplants (unpeeled),
    thinly sliced lengthwise
1 teaspoon red pepper flakes
1 cup freshly grated fontina
    cheese

2 cups freshly grated
    mozzarella cheese
1 cup cubed goat cheese
4 ounces thinly sliced Black
    Forest Ham, julienned
1 bunch fresh basil, chopped
1 basic pizza dough recipe

Preheat oven to 475 degrees. Heat ¼ cup olive oil in skillet on medium high heat and sauté eggplant until lightly browned, about 2 minutes. Drain on paper towel. Brush each pizza with ½ tablespoon olive oil. Sprinkle with red pepper flakes, fontina, mozzarella, eggplant, goat cheese, ham and basil. Bake on pizza stone for 10 to 12 minutes. May be frozen. Serves 4.

GORGONZOLA, LEEK AND RICOTTA PIZZA

1 medium onion, finely
chopped
2 tablespoons olive oil
1 28-ounce can recipe ready
chopped tomatoes in
juice
2 tablespoons tomato paste
1 clove garlic, minced
1 teaspoon dried oregano
1 teaspoon dried basil
1 bay leaf

freshly ground pepper to
taste
1 large prepared pizza crust
2 leeks, thinly sliced, white
part only
olive oil
1 cup ricotta cheese
1 cup bleu cheese, or
Gorgonzola cheese,
crumbled
2 cups mozzarella cheese,
grated

Preheat oven to 450 degrees. In a 3-quart stainless steel sauce-pan, lightly sauté the onions in olive oil over medium heat until translucent. Add tomatoes and tomato paste to onions. Add garlic and seasonings and reduce to simmer. Stir occasionally and simmer sauce, uncovered, for approximately 20 to 30 minutes. While sauce us simmering, sauté leeks in a covered skillet (that has been coated with ⅛-inch olive oil) until leeks are tender. When sauce is done, spoon ½ of sauce onto pizza crust. Remaining ½ sauce may be frozen. Layer leeks on top of sauce, then spoon ricotta cheese onto pizza, spreading it a little bit as you spoon it onto pizza. Next, sprinkle bleu cheese or Gorgonzola over ricotta and top with grated mozzarella. Bake for 10 minutes (preferably on a pizza stone), and serve. Serves 4 adults.

TORTELLINI AND ARTICHOKE SALAD

1 10-ounce package fresh
cheese or chicken
tortellini
6 marinated artichoke hearts,
drained and quartered
(reserve liquid)
2 to 3 tablespoons diced
roasted red peppers
4 tablespoons reduced calorie
mayonnaise

2 teaspoons Dijon mustard
1 tablespoon grated
Parmesan cheese
salt
white pepper
2 tablespoons fresh sweet
basil, cut into slivers (or
1½ teaspoons dried)
2 tablespoons chopped Italian
parsley

Cook tortellini as directed on package. Rinse with cold water and drain well. Toss with 1 tablespoon marinated artichoke liquid (or olive oil) to keep from sticking together. Refrigerate tortellini while preparing rest of ingredients. Drain artichokes and cut into quarters. Combine cooled tortellini, artichokes and red peppers with mayonnaise, mustard, salt and pepper. Refrigerate until served. Garnish with fresh basil just before serving. Variation: Add 1 cup small, cooked shrimp, or slivers of prosciutto. Serves 4 for luncheon, or 6 for appetizer.

QUICK DELICIOUS PASTA

½ pound spinach, tomato, or
plain fettucine
8 ounces Boursin cheese (use
either Boursin cheese
with herbs and garlic, or
Boursin cheese with
pepper)

4 tablespoons milk
¼ teaspoon red pepper
red and green bell pepper
strips

Cook pasta. Melt cheese, red pepper and milk over low heat. Drain pasta, pour cheese mixture on top and toss. Garnish with bell pepper strips for color. Serves 4.

NOODLE MUSHROOM SALAD

Sesame-Ginger Dressing:
½ cup vegetable oil
6 tablespoons white distilled
   vinegar
4 tablespoons water

3 tablespoons freshly grated
   ginger root (or 2
   teaspoons dry ginger)
2 teaspoons hot pepper sauce
4 tablespoons sesame seeds,
   toasted

Salad:
8 ounces fine egg noodles
1 pound fresh mushrooms,
   thickly sliced
8 green onions with tops,
   chopped coarsely

1 medium sweet red pepper,
   seeded and cut into short
   strips
½ cup chopped parsley

To make dressing, place in blender container all dressing ingredients except sesame seeds. Blend until well mixed. Toast 4 tablespoons of sesame seeds in a dry skillet until they turn golden. When the seeds are cool, add to the dressing and mix. Set aside. Cook noodles as directed on package and rinse immediately with cold running water. Drain noodles thoroughly. In large bowl mix the noodles, mushrooms, green onion, red pepper and parsley. Add the prepared dressing, toss again, then set aside for about 10 minutes at room temperature to marinate. Garnish with more parsley or toast some additional sesame seeds and garnish salad with them. Serve on pretty lettuce leaf-lined platter. Serves 8.

Reheating Pasta: *Successfully reheating pasta has been made possible with the microwave oven. The microwaves affect only the water molecules, thereby warming the pasta without drying it out. Microwave pasta in a covered dish on HIGH POWER for about a minute. If still cold stir and continue a minute. If still cold stir and continue on HIGH for 15 second intervals, checking to see if warmed through. Another method is to wrap the pasta in aluminum foil and reheat in a 350 degree oven for 15 to 20 minutes.*

ZUCCHINI-SHRIMP PASTA

2 tablespoons olive oil
½ pound raw shrimp, peeled
  and deveined
4 medium zucchini, cut into
  1 x ¼-inch pieces
1 package refrigerated fresh
  linguine

¼ to ½ teaspoon red pepper
  flakes
1 clove garlic, halved
2 to 3 tablespoons margarine
2 to 3 tablespoons fresh
  grated Parmesan

Heat olive oil in large skillet and add garlic. Sauté until garlic begins to brown, then discard garlic. Add zucchini to oil and stir often until softened and beginning to brown. Add shrimp and red pepper flakes, stirring often until shrimp are firm and pink. Cook linguine according to package directions. Drain and toss lightly with margarine and Parmesan. Layer linguine with shrimp/zucchini mixture, ending with shrimp/zucchini mixture. Top with fresh grated Parmesan and serve. Helpful hints: Have water for pasta boiling, and cook the pasta when adding shrimp to zucchini. All will be ready at the same time. Also, when layering linguine and shrimp/zucchini mixture, layer into individual serving bowls. Variation: Excellent with calamata Greek olives and broccoli florets instead of shrimp and zucchini. Serves 2-4.

FETTUCINE WITH GARDEN VEGGIES

¼ cup margarine
1 12-ounce package baby
  carrots, peeled
1 medium size onion, diced
1 8-ounce package spinach
  fettucine noodles
4 ounces Chinese pea pods
1 cup sliced fresh mushrooms

1 clove garlic, minced
1½ teaspoons dried basil leaves
½ cup heavy cream
½ cup freshly grated
  Parmesan cheese
1½ teaspoons salt
½ teaspoon freshly ground
  pepper

In saucepan over high heat, bring water to boil and cook fettucine. Meanwhile, in large skillet over medium heat, melt margarine. Add carrots and onion. Cook 5 minutes, stirring occasionally. Add pea pods, mushrooms, garlic and basil to skillet. Cook 5 minutes, stirring occasionally until vegetables are crisp-tender. Drain pasta. Add to skillet along with cream, grated Parmesan cheese, salt and pepper. Cook about 1 minute, stirring until heated through. Serve hot with salad and French bread or bread sticks. Serves 6.

Poultry

Canton First Monday Trade Days

A trip to Canton during the First Monday Trade Days is an eclectic adventure of arts and crafts, antiques, food, clothing and collectibles.

Each month more than five thousand dealers come together to "set up shop." Unique and "one of a kind" wares such as twig furniture, primitives and antique tools can be found as one meanders through the multitude of shops and vendor stalls.

While enjoying this festive country atmosphere, try the famous Trade Days lemonade, turkey legs and funnel cakes.

SEALED IN SILVER

Seasoned Butter:

¼ cup packed Italian parsley
1 clove garlic
4 tablespoons unsalted
butter, softened

¼ teaspoon salt
½ teaspoon pepper
¼ teaspoon dried tarragon,
crumbled

Other Ingredients:

celery, carrots, sweet red
pepper or parsnips, cut
into julienned strips
salt and pepper to taste

4 boneless, skinless chicken
breasts, fully thawed and
flattened
regular weight foil

Preheat oven to 400 degrees. Finely chop parsley and garlic in food processor. Add other ingredients and process to blend well. Tear off 4 sheets of **REGULAR WEIGHT FOIL**, 12 x 11 inches each. Place a flattened chicken breast on each sheet. Spread with seasoned butter. Place julienned vegetables of your choice over chicken and sprinkle with salt and pepper to taste. Seal foil tightly. Place pockets in single layer on a preheated baking pan, 1 inch apart, folded side up. Bake 30-35 minutes. Serves 4.

ITALIAN STYLE BAKED CHICKEN

2 to 2½ pounds fryer
chickens, quartered
salt
pepper
1 cup corn flakes (crumbs)
⅓ cup grated Parmesan
cheese

2 teaspoons dried oregano
leaves
1 can condensed tomato soup
⅓ cup water
¼ cup butter or margarine,
melted
3 tablespoons milk

Preheat oven to 400 degrees. Sprinkle chicken with salt and pepper. Mix corn flake crumbs, Parmesan cheese and oregano. Mix soup and water together. Dip chicken in soup mixture, then thoroughly coat with crumbs. Save any left over soup to use in gravy. Pour melted butter into a 3-quart shallow baking dish. Place chicken in dish, skin side up. Bake 55 - 60 minutes, or until tender with fork. Remove to platter. Pour drippings into saucepan. Add remaining soup mixture and milk. Stir and serve over chicken. Add additional milk for thinner sauce. Serves 6-8.

CHICKEN SPAGHETTI

10 chicken breasts
1 16-ounce box spaghetti
1 6-ounce can tomato paste
1 28-ounce can chopped
    tomatoes
2 tablespoons oil
2 green peppers, chopped
2 stalks celery, chopped
3 medium onions, chopped
3 cloves garlic

1 8-ounce can mushrooms,
    sliced
1 small jar pimento, chopped
1 1-pound block processed
    cheese, cubed
1 16-ounce jar processed
    cheese
2 cups Cheddar cheese (for
    topping)

Cook chicken breasts in seasoned water until tender; cool and cut into bite-size pieces. Cook spaghetti in chicken broth for 10-11 minutes. Drain and reserve extra broth. While cooking spaghetti, mix tomato paste and chopped tomatoes. In oil, sauté peppers, celery, onions and garlic. Combine with tomato paste and chopped tomatoes. Add mushrooms, pimento, cubed cheese and processed cheese. Mix thoroughly and put into a 9 x 13 x 2-inch oiled rectangular dish. Top with shredded cheese and bake in a 350 degree oven until bubbly, about 30 minutes. Serves 10-12.

CHICKEN SCALOPPINI

4 boneless, skinless chicken
    breasts
3 tablespoons flour
1 teaspoon salt
⅛ teaspoon pepper
3 tablespoons olive oil

1 clove garlic
1 thin slice lemon
½ cup onion, sliced
4 ounces mushrooms, sliced
½ cup white table wine
½ cup water

Combine flour, salt and pepper. Pound chicken thin. Coat chicken in flour mixture. Heat oil over medium heat. Add garlic and chicken. Brown on both sides. Remove garlic and reduce heat. Add lemon, onion and mushrooms. Combine wine and water and add ⅓ of it. Cover and simmer on low for 25 minutes. Add remaining wine and water as needed to keep sauce simmering. Serves 4.

CHICKEN PAPRIKASH

3 tablespoons olive oil
1 onion, chopped
1 chicken, cut into serving
    portions, or 2 pounds
    boneless, skinless
    chicken breasts plus ½
    pound chicken wings
1 tablespoon paprika
    (Hungarian style
    recommended)
1-2 teaspoons hot Hungarian
    paprika or other hot red
    pepper

¼ teaspoon salt
¼ teaspoon pepper
1 whole allspice berry
1 bay leaf
1 clove garlic, chopped
1½ cups chicken broth
1 chicken bouillon cube
¼ cup flour mixed in ¼ cup
    water
½ cup sour cream (optional)

NOKY (pronounced *naukee*):
1 egg
1 cup milk or water

2 cups flour
1 teaspoon salt

To prepare chicken: Cook onion in oil until transparent. Remove from pan. Sprinkle chicken on both sides with paprika mixture and brown in remaining oil. Replace onions and add salt, pepper, allspice berry, bay leaf and garlic. To this, add chicken broth and bouillon mixture. Cover and simmer until tender, about 45 minutes. Transfer chicken to a warm serving platter. Remove allspice berry and bay leaf; add flour and water mixture to remaining liquid. Stir and check seasoning. Add more salt and paprika if needed. Simmer 5 minutes. Just before serving, add sour cream. Place chicken over NOKY or rice and pour sauce over all to serve.
To prepare NOKY (pronounced *naukee*): Blend egg, milk, flour and salt with fork. Let set 10-20 minutes. Drop by teaspoonfuls into boiling water. To prevent batter from sticking to spoon, dip spoon into boiling water before spooning batter. When NOKY rises to top, it is done. Check for doneness by cutting in half. Middle should be firm. Use strainer to lift out in 2 or 3 batches. Serves 4.

GRILLED CHICKEN WITH CABBAGE ANCHOYADE

8 strips lemon peel, removed with vegetable peeler
2 teaspoons black peppercorns
4 tablespoons fresh oregano

4 boneless, skinless chicken breasts from roasting chickens (about 8 ounces each)
3 tablespoons virgin olive oil
1 teaspoon salt

Cabbage Anchoyade:
4 cloves garlic, peeled, crushed and finely chopped (about 2 teaspoons)
6 anchovy fillets, finely chopped (4 teaspoons)
½ teaspoon salt

½ teaspoon freshly ground black pepper
½ red bell pepper, cut into ¼-inch dice (½ cup)
4 teaspoons red wine vinegar
4 tablespoons virgin olive oil
18 ounces Savoy cabbage, shredded (8 cups)

To Prepare Cabbage: Combine garlic, anchovies, salt, pepper, red bell pepper (reserving 1 tablespoon for garnish), vinegar, oil and cabbage in bowl. Mix well. Can be made 3 to 4 hours ahead of time. Refrigerate until serving time. To Prepare Chicken: Place the lemon strips, peppercorns and oregano in the bowl of a mini-chopper, and process to a powder (about 4 tablespoons). Arrange chicken in a dish and sprinkle the lemon mixture over the chicken. Drizzle with olive oil. Cover and place in refrigerator to marinate overnight. At cooking time, sprinkle the chicken with salt and arrange on hot grill. Cook about 4 minutes on each side, and transfer to warm oven (180 degrees) until serving time (up to 1 hour ahead). To serve, arrange cabbage mixture in a mound in center of four serving plates. Slice chicken breasts lengthwise and arrange the meat all around and on top of cabbage. Sprinkle with reserved red bell pepper and serve immediately. Serves 4.

CHICKEN MARBELLA

4 chickens, 2½ pounds each, skinned and quartered, or substitute 8 pounds fresh chicken breasts
1 head of garlic, peeled and finely pureed
¼ cup dried oregano
coarse salt and freshly ground black pepper to taste
½ cup red wine vinegar
½ cup olive oil
1 cup pitted prunes
½ cup pitted Spanish green olives
½ cup capers with a bit of juice
6 bay leaves
1 cup brown sugar
1 cup white wine
¼ cup Italian parsley finely chopped

In a large bowl, combine chicken quarters or chicken breasts, garlic, oregano, pepper and coarse salt to taste, vinegar, olive oil, prunes, olives, capers and juice, and bay leaves. Cover and let marinate, refrigerated, overnight (save marinade). Preheat oven to 350 degrees. Arrange chicken in a single layer in one or two large, shallow baking pans and spoon marinade over it evenly. Sprinkle chicken pieces with brown sugar and pour white wine around them. Bake for 45 minutes to 1 hour, basting frequently with pan juices. Chicken is done when thigh pieces, pricked with a fork at their thickest, yield clear yellow (rather than pink) juice. With a slotted spoon transfer chicken, prunes, olives and capers to a serving platter. Moisten with a few spoonfuls of pan juices and sprinkle generously with parsley or cilantro. Pass remaining pan juices in a sauceboat. To serve cold, cool to room temperature in cooking juices before transferring to a serving platter. If chicken has been covered and refrigerated, allow it to return to room temperature before serving. Spoon some of the reserved juice over chicken. Serves 10-12.

CHICKEN BREASTS TARRAGON

4 pounds chicken breasts
2 tablespoons oil
2 tablespoons butter
6 shallots, chopped
2 pared carrots, sliced ¼-inch
¼ cup cognac
1 cup dry white wine
2 teaspoons dried tarragon
½ teaspoon dried chervil
½ teaspoon salt
⅛ teaspoon pepper
1 cup light cream
1 egg yolk
1 tablespoon flour
¼ pound fresh mushrooms, sliced
sprigs of fresh tarragon

In Dutch oven, heat oil and butter. Brown chicken breasts. Remove. Add carrots and shallots to drippings. Sauté 5 minutes. Return chicken. Heat cognac. When hot, ignite and pour over chicken. Add wine, chopped tarragon, chervil, salt and pepper. Bring to boil. Reduce heat and simmer 30 minutes. Remove chicken to serving platter. Discard vegetables. Combine cream, egg yolk and flour, and mix well with wire whisk until sauce thickens. Sauté mushrooms. Garnish plate with tarragon sprigs and mushrooms. Serves 8.

LIME CHICKEN

finely grated peel and juice of
    1 lime
3 tablespoons brown sugar
1 chicken, cut into serving
    pieces
⅓ cup flour
1½ teaspoons salt
½ teaspoon pepper
¼ cup vegetable oil
½ cup chicken broth
½ cup dry white wine
fresh mint
1 lime
1 avocado, sliced

Sprinkle lime juice over chicken. Shake chicken pieces in paper bag with flour, salt and pepper. Brown in oil. Arrange in single layer in baking dish. Combine lime peel with brown sugar and sprinkle over chicken. Add broth and wine. Place sprig of mint on each piece. Bake at 375 degrees for 45 minutes to 1 hour. Cut thin wedges from second lime. Squeeze rest of lime over avocado to prevent darkening. Chill. When chicken is tender, transfer to warm platter, discarding mint. Garnish with lime wedges, avocado crescents and more fresh mint. Serves 4.

POLLO DEL SOL

1 chicken, cut into 8 serving
  pieces
3 tablespoons olive oil
4 cloves garlic, minced
1 onion, finely chopped
¾ cup dry white wine

1 small lemon, thinly sliced
  and seeds removed
12 Italian dried olives
4 sun-dried or oven-dried
  tomatoes, slivered

Blot chicken pieces with paper towels until they are dry. Heat olive oil in a large skillet. When olive oil is very hot, but not smoking, sauté the pieces of chicken, skin side down. Sauté 10 minutes on one side and 5 minutes on the other side. Remove chicken from skillet and set aside. Using the same oil in skillet, cook garlic and onions over medium heat for 5 minutes, or until onions are tender. Over high heat, add wine and all chicken parts except breast. Add salt and pepper to taste, cover and simmer for 15 minutes. After 15 minutes, turn chicken pieces over and add breasts, lemon slices, tomatoes and olives. Cover and cook 15 minutes. Remove chicken from skillet and arrange on platter. Turn up heat and quickly reduce the liquid until it starts to become syrupy. Spoon it and the tomatoes, lemon and olives over the chicken pieces and serve. Serves 4.

CHICKEN SOUR CREAM ENCHILADAS

1 pint sour cream
2 cans cream of chicken soup
1 4-ounce can chopped green
  chilies
½ medium onion, chopped
1 pound cheese (Colby Jack,
  Cheddar, Monterey Jack),
  grated

4-5 chicken breasts, cooked
  and diced
1 small package corn tortillas
green onions, chopped
seeded tomatoes, finely
  chopped, for garnish

Prepare the sauce by mixing half the amount of each: sour cream, soup, chilies, onion and cheese. Set aside. Mix together remaining sour cream, soup, chilies, chicken, onion and cheese for filling. Heat tortillas until soft. Roll enchiladas with 2-3 tablespoons chicken filling. Arrange in a 9 x 13-inch baking dish. Top with sauce and chopped green onions for color if desired. Bake at 325 degrees for 30 minutes, or until sauce bubbles. Top with finely-chopped, seeded tomatoes for added garnish. Serves 8.

CHICKEN ALOUETTE

1 17¼-ounce package frozen
puff pastry, thawed
4 ounces garlic and spice
alouette cheese

6 skinned and boned chicken
breasts, flattened
½ teaspoon salt
⅛ teaspoon pepper
1 egg, beaten

Unfold pastry sheets and roll each sheet into a 14 x 12-inch rectangle on a lightly floured surface. Cut one sheet into four 7 x 6-inch rectangles. Cut second sheet into two 7 x 6-inch rectangles and one 12 x 6-inch rectangle. Set large rectangle aside. Shape each small rectangle into an oval by trimming off corners. Spread pastry ovals evenly with cheese. Sprinkle chicken with salt and pepper; place one chicken breast in center of each pastry oval. Lightly moisten edges with water. Fold ends over chicken; fold sides over and press to seal. Place each bundle, seal side down, on a lightly sprayed baking sheet. Cut remaining pastry into 12 x ¼-inch strips. Braid 2 strips and place crosswise over chicken bundles. Braid 2 more and place lengthwise over bundles, trimming and tucking ends under. Repeat procedure with remaining strips, or cut out a favorite design (holly leaf, etc.). Cover and refrigerate for up to 2 hours if desired. Return to room temperature before baking. Combine egg and water; brush on bundles. Bake at 350 degrees for about 25 to 30 minutes, or until done. It may be necessary to cover design on pastry with foil for the first 15 minutes, so that they will not brown too quickly. Serves 6.

Canton, Texas, is the home of "First Monday Trade Days" — but those in the know start arriving by as early as 11:00 A.M. on the Thursday preceding the first Monday of each month. Friday, Saturday and Sunday shoppers looking for the best buys arrive by 8:30 A.M. Many come at later times to leisurely stroll the aisles and to simply experience this massive East Texas phenomenon. It is said that in October, 1993, as many as 200,000 people attended in one weekend.

HEARTY CHICKEN WITH FETA, SUN-DRIED TOMATOES AND BASIL

½ cup flour
½ teaspoon lite salt
½ teaspoon dried marjoram
  leaves
½ teaspoon dried oregano
½ teaspoon white pepper
6-8 chicken breasts, skinless
  and boneless
¼ cup extra virgin olive oil
1 cup low sodium chicken
  broth
2 tablespoons lemon juice,
  freshly squeezed

2 cups Roma tomatoes,
  peeled, seeded and
  chopped
24 Kalamata olives
1 clove garlic, pressed
½ pound feta cheese
2 tablespoons sun-dried
  tomatoes
¼ cup fresh basil leaves, cut
  up (use scissors)
fresh whole leaves of basil
  for garnish

Combine flour, salt, marjoram, oregano and pepper. Blend well. Coat chicken in mixture, reserving what is left. In a large fry pan, heat oil and brown chicken on both sides. Remove chicken to a platter. Reduce heat, drain off all but a tablespoon of liquid. Stir 3 tablespoons of the reserved flour mixture into oil and mix well with a wire whisk. Add broth and lemon juice slowly, mixing well again with a whisk. When thickened and smooth, add tomatoes, olives and garlic. Return chicken to pan and spoon sauce over all parts. Cover and cook 30 to 40 minutes over medium low heat. Check frequently for sticking. Mix feta cheese, sun-dried tomatoes and basil together. Sprinkle on top of chicken and cook until cheese melts. Remove from pan and arrange on platter. Garnish with fresh basil. Serves 6-8.

CHICKEN MOUSSAKA

4 tablespoons olive oil
1 medium sweet onion,
    chopped
1 clove garlic, peeled and
    crushed
1 pound raw chicken,
    chopped
2 tablespoons tomato puree
1 cup chicken broth
2 tablespoons fresh parsley,
    chopped

salt and pepper to taste
pinch of nutmeg
2 medium eggplants, peeled
    and thinly sliced
¼ pint yogurt
1 egg
2 tablespoons mozzarella
    cheese, grated
1 tablespoon Parmesan
    cheese, grated

Heat half of oil; sauté onion and garlic. Add chicken and lightly brown. Add tomato puree, chicken broth, parsley and seasonings. Cover and simmer gently for 10 minutes. Place eggplant slices on lightly sprayed baking sheets. Brush with remaining oil. Bake in oven for 8 minutes at 350 degrees. Remove from oven. In lightly oiled 13 x 9 x 2-inch dish, place a layer of eggplant and then a layer of chicken. Repeat layers. Beat yogurt with egg and mozzarella cheese. Add to top and sprinkle with Parmesan cheese. Return to 350 degree oven for 15 - 20 minutes, or until top is brown. Slice in squares. Serve hot. Serves 6.

CRUNCHY CHICKEN

2 fryers, cut into serving
    pieces, *or* 8 chicken
    breasts
2 cups Ritz cracker crumbs,
    or 1½ cups bread crumbs
¾ cup Parmesan cheese

¼ cup parsley
1 teaspoon salt
2 cloves garlic, minced
¼ teaspoon pepper
1 cup butter, melted

Preheat oven to 350 degrees. Blend Ritz crumbs, Parmesan cheese and seasonings. Dip chicken pieces in butter, then in crumb mixture. Place in baking pan and drizzle any remaining butter over chicken. Bake for 1 hour if using chicken with bones; 30-40 minutes if using boneless chicken. Serves 8.

SINGAPORE CHICKEN

½ cup flour
½ teaspoon salt
¼ teaspoon pepper
1 3½-pound chicken, cut up,
  or 5 - 6 boneless breasts
2-3 tablespoons butter
1 can green beans, drained, or
  9 ounces fresh snow peas

½ cup chopped onion
1 can cream of mushroom
  soup
⅓ cup milk
2 tablespoons soy sauce
½ teaspoon ground ginger
1 3-ounce can chow mein
  noodles

Preheat oven to 375 degrees. Combine flour, salt and pepper in baggie. Shake chicken until coated. Heat butter in skillet and brown chicken on both sides. Remove and place in 2-quart casserole. Sprinkle beans over chicken. Sauté onions in skillet with butter residue; add soy sauce, soup, milk and ginger. Simmer and stir, scraping up all bits in skillet for 1 to 2 minutes. Pour over chicken in casserole dish and bake, covered, 45 minutes. Uncover, and top with noodles. Bake for another 10 minutes.

SWISS ENCHILADAS

1 yellow onion, chopped
2 tablespoons oil
2 cloves garlic, crushed
2 10½-ounce cans tomato
  puree
1 can green chilies, chopped
3 cups cooked chicken,
  chopped

salt and pepper to taste
1 dozen flour tortillas
3 cups half and half
1 tablespoon chicken-
  seasoned stock base
sour cream
Monterey Jack cheese

Preheat oven to 325 degrees. To prepare filling, sauté onion in oil until soft but not browned. Add garlic, tomato puree, chilies, chicken, salt and pepper. Simmer about 10 minutes. Warm tortillas on griddle. Do not let them become crisp. Heat half and half, and dissolve chicken seasoned stock base in it. Dip each tortilla into cream mixture and fill with 2 tablespoonfuls of chicken mixture and roll. Arrange in baking dish with loose edges down, and pour remaining cream mixture over them. Top with grated cheese and bake for about 30 minutes, or until cheese is melted and ingredients are heated thoroughly. Garnish with sour cream and fresh cilantro when serving. Serves 6.

GRILLED LIME CHICKEN

3 pounds chicken pieces
(breast, thigh, etc.)
lime juice from 6-8 limes
paprika

seasoning salt
4 tablespoons butter
1 teaspoon Worcestershire
pepper to taste

Squeeze lime juice on each side of chicken parts. Sprinkle each side with pepper, seasoning salt and paprika. Marinate in refrigerator for at least 30 minutes if you are using thighs or single breast, longer if you are using broiler halves, or other large pieces. Baste and turn occasionally. Melt butter; add juice of 2 or 3 limes, Worcestershire sauce and marinating juice. Brush chicken with sauce and cook over medium coals on grill, continuing to brush chicken as it cooks. A wonderful, tangy dish. Serves 6.

VERMICELLI E POLLO

4-5 boneless chicken breast
halves
6-8 tablespoons butter
½ pound fresh mushrooms,
sliced
7 tablespoons flour
2 cups chicken stock
1 cup milk
¼ cup white wine

1 clove garlic, mashed
1 cup heavy cream
¼ cup sour cream
salt and pepper to taste
1 9-ounce package fresh
fettuccine
4 tablespoons bread crumbs
4 tablespoons freshly grated
Parmesan cheese

Cut chicken in bite-size pieces and sauté in 2 tablespoons butter until opaque. Remove from pan. Sauté mushrooms and garlic until done, adding more butter as needed. Remove from pan. Melt 4 tablespoons butter and add flour. Mix well with whisk. Whisk in stock, wine and milk. Cook until thickened, then simmer for 3 minutes. Remove from heat and stir in heavy cream, sour cream, salt and pepper. Add chicken and mushrooms to sauce mixture, mixing well. Combine sauce and cooked pasta. Place all in buttered casserole. Sprinkle top with Parmesan and bread crumbs. Bake at 350 degrees for 20 - 30 minutes. Serves 6-8.

SPINACH-FILLED TURKEY OR CHICKEN ROLL

1½ pounds ground turkey
½ cup onion, finely chopped
1 cup homemade tomato
    sauce (recipe follows)
2 slices bread, crumbled
2 eggs, slightly beaten
1 teaspoon dry mustard
½ teaspoon salt

½ teaspoon oregano leaves
¼ teaspoon garlic powder
1 9-ounce package frozen
    spinach, chopped,
    thawed and squeezed dry
2 ounces shredded part-skim
    mozzarella cheese

Homemade Tomato Sauce:
2 cups onions, chopped
2 garlic cloves, minced
⅓ cups olive oil
8 cups tomatoes, peeled and
    coarsely chopped
1 tablespoon oregano leaves,
    chopped
1 teaspoon sugar

1 teaspoon basil leaves,
    minced
1 teaspoon rosemary, crushed
½ teaspoon salt
¼ teaspoon pepper
2 cups water
1 12-ounce can tomato paste

To Prepare Tomato Sauce: Sauté onion and garlic in olive oil in large pan. Add remaining ingredients and bring to boil, stirring occasionally. Reduce heat; simmer uncovered 1 hour, stirring occasionally. (May freeze in small portions for later use.) To Prepare Turkey Roll: Preheat oven to 350 degrees. Combine turkey, onion, tomato sauce, bread crumbs, eggs, mustard, oregano, garlic powder and salt; mix thoroughly. On sheet of foil, pat mixture out to 12 x 8-inch rectangle. Spread spinach over meat mixture, and sprinkle with cheese. Starting with 8-inch side, roll up (lift foil to help). Place roll, seam side down, on foil on ungreased jellyroll pan. Bake at 350 degrees for 55 to 65 minutes. Let stand 10 minutes. Heat tomato sauce; serve with turkey roll. Freezes and reheats well. Serves 6-8.

EASY CHICKEN CURRY

½ cup green onions, chopped
2 tablespoons butter
1 can cream of chicken soup
½ can water

1 teaspoon curry powder
3 chicken breasts, boneless
and skinless, sliced into
½-inch strips

Sauté onions in butter. Add soup, curry powder and raw sliced chicken strips. Cook in saucepan uncovered until chicken is done. Serve over rice with curry condiments such as chutney, chopped cashews, and chopped green onions. This may be multiplied to desired amount. When doing so, add flour when sautéing onions so that soup will not be too thin. Add 1 tablespoon flour for each multiple above one recipe. Serves 3.

HONEY GLAZED BAKED CHICKEN

8 split chicken breasts,
boneless and skinless
8 tablespoons margarine
½ cup onion, chopped
2 large garlic cloves, minced
¼ cup Dijon mustard

½ cup mild honey
1 teaspoon salt
1 teaspoon curry powder
1 tablespoon chutney, dried
currants or chopped
raisins

Preheat oven to 350 degrees. Melt margarine in large skillet. Sauté onion and garlic until tender. Add remaining ingredients and bring to boil. Place chicken in baking pan. Pour sauce over chicken and bake for about 40 to 45 minutes at 350 degrees. Serves 6-8.

GRILLED CORNISH HENS WITH ORANGE GLAZE

2 Cornish hens, halved
¼ cup Grand Marnier
1 cup fresh orange juice
1 tablespoon ginger, freshly
   grated

2 cloves garlic, peeled and
   minced
zest of 1 lemon
juice of 1 lemon

Place hens in container with a cover. Combine remaining ingredients and pour over hens. Marinate overnight in refrigerator. Turn over from time to time to ensure that marinade covers well. Remove hens, place marinade in pan and reduce over high heat until syrupy. Grill hens over medium hot coals, 1 to 2 minutes per side. Cover grill and cook hens 8 to 10 minutes. Baste frequently with sauce. Serves 4.

ORIENTAL GRILLED CHICKEN

2 teaspoons Szechwan
   peppercorns
1 3½- to 4-pound chicken,
   cut up
1 clove garlic, minced

1 tablespoon fresh ginger,
   minced
1 tablespoon dark soy sauce
2 tablespoons sesame oil
¼ cup fresh cilantro leaves,
   chopped

Toast peppercorns in small pan over medium heat for 5 minutes, or until they begin to smoke. Cool and crush finely with mortar and pestle. Wash and wipe chicken dry with paper towels. Combine peppercorn powder, garlic, ginger, soy sauce, sesame oil and cilantro. Mix well and coat chicken. Marinate at least 2 hours in refrigerator. Grill or broil chicken, and serve with fried rice and snow peas. Serves 6.

MARINATED DOVE BREASTS

8 dove breasts, removed from
    bone
1 apple, peeled, cored and cut
    into 8 slices

8 strips bacon
½ cup red wine

Soy-Ginger Marinade:
½ cup soy sauce
½ teaspoon garlic powder,
    or 1 fresh garlic clove,
    crushed

½ teaspoon powdered ginger
1 cup red wine

Combine marinade ingredients. Add doves, cover and refrigerate overnight. Remove from marinade. Place an apple slice inside each breast. Fold breast over apple. Wrap a strip of bacon around each and secure with toothpick. Place in casserole and add wine. Bake at 350 degrees for 30 minutes, or until tender. Baste and remove toothpicks. Serves 4-6.

WHITE CHILI

1 tablespoon salad oil
1 medium onion, chopped
1 clove garlic, minced
1 teaspoon ground cumin
2 whole large chicken
    breasts, cubed
1 can white kidney beans

1 can garbanzo beans
1 can white corn
2 4-ounce cans chopped
    green chilies
2 chicken flavored bouillon
    cubes
Monterey Jack cheese

Preheat oven to 350 degrees. Sauté onion with garlic and cumin. In 2½-quart casserole, combine onion mixture with chicken, beans, corn, chilies, bouillon and 1½ cups water. Bake 1 hour, or until chicken is tender. Serves 4.

CHICKEN MARINADE

1 cup cooking oil
1 pint vinegar
3 tablespoons salt

1 tablespoon poultry
  seasoning
1 teaspoon pepper
1 egg

In a quart jar with lid, place egg and remaining ingredients and shake. Pour over meat at least 6 hours before grilling.

SUNDAY NIGHT HASH

2 cups basic white sauce
  (or Mornay or Mustard
  Sauce)
1 cup diced cooked chicken
½ cup sautéed mushrooms
½ cup diced pimento

½ cup slivered almonds,
  toasted
½ teaspoon pepper
salt to taste
thin ham slices (if desired)

Mix and heat in skillet. Serve on toasted bread or English muffins on which thinly sliced ham has been placed. Also delicious over wild or white rice. Serves 4.

HOMEMADE CHICKEN STOCK

Careful cooks insist on using only **Homemade Chicken Stock***.
Here's how to make it best.*

4 to 5 pounds chicken with
  bones and skin
3 quarts water
1 teaspoon salt, or more to
  taste
1 large or 2 medium onions
4 ribs celery with leaves

8 sprigs fresh dill
3 cloves garlic, quartered
4 carrots, peeled
3 leeks or parsnips, peeled
freshly ground pepper to
  taste

Rinse chicken and place in large soup pot with water and salt. Bring to a boil and skim off foam as it forms. Add onions, celery, dill, carrots, and leeks or parsnips. Reduce the heat and simmer (LOW) for 2 hours. Remove chicken, discard carrots and leeks. Strain stock and allow to cool. Refrigerate or freeze. To reduce to richer stock, cook on MEDIUM HIGH until reduces by half.

Salads and Dressings

Longview Great Texas Balloon Race

Up, up and away! This action-packed event is held at Longview's Gregg County Airport each July where balloonists come from across the state to compete.

The famous Balloon Glow, which originated in Longview, is an enchanting event with the sky ablaze in dazzling colors and shapes. The entire family will thrill at the sight of over 90 spectacular hot air balloons.

Along with these sensational aerial displays are activities for children, entertainment and tailgating for a hot summer day!

ASPARAGUS A LA CRÈME

40 fresh asparagus spears, well trimmed
2 tablespoons shallots, minced
2 tablespoons Dijon mustard
1 tablespoon sour cream or crème fraîche
1 tablespoon red wine vinegar
salt and pepper to taste
½ cup peanut oil
lettuce

Steam asparagus until barely crisp-tender. Set aside to cool. Combine next 4 ingredients with salt and pepper in small bowl and blend with whisk. Slowly add oil a spoonful at a time, beating constantly until thoroughly mixed and thickened. Line plates with lettuce and divide asparagus evenly. Drizzle with vinaigrette. Serve immediately, or chilled. Serve with Crème Fraîche. Serves 8.

Crème Fraîche:
1 tablespoon buttermilk to 1 cup heavy cream

Heat to lukewarm. Let stand overnight at room temperature, then refrigerate.

FIESTA GUACAMOLE

8 avocados, diced
2 cups green onions, chopped
2 cups fresh tomatoes, peeled, seeded and diced
juice of ½ lime
1 cup picante sauce
½ teaspoon salt
4 tablespoons fresh cilantro, minced (optional)
¼ cup Best Salad Dressing (see Salads And Dressings)
tortilla chips

Mix first 3 ingredients together. Add lime juice, picante, salt and cilantro. Serve with tortilla chips as an appetizer, or with lettuce as a salad with vinaigrette dressing. As an appetizer, serves 15-20.

AVOCADO AND SHRIMP SALAD

3 tablespoons olive oil
2 tablespoons white wine
  vinegar
1 teaspoon Dijon mustard
1 pound fresh shrimp,
  cooked, shelled, deveined
  and cubed
1 cup mayonnaise
2 tablespoons chili sauce
1 large garlic clove, crushed
Tabasco to taste

salt and freshly ground
  pepper
1 large ripe avocado
juice of ½ lemon
2 tablespoons fresh dill,
  finely minced
2 tablespoons fresh chives,
  finely minced
dill sprigs, lemon wedges and
  avocado slices to garnish

Whisk together olive oil, white wine vinegar and Dijon mustard until well blended. Add shrimp, toss thoroughly, cover and marinate for at least one hour. Meanwhile, whisk mayonnaise, chili sauce, garlic, Tabasco, salt and pepper until smooth. Set aside. Peel, pit and cube avocado. Sprinkle with lemon juice. Drain shrimp. Add cubed avocado, dill and chives, and toss lightly. Fold in enough mayonnaise mixture to coat lightly. Taste and adjust seasoning. Cover and chill until ready to serve. Divide salad among chilled plates and garnish with dill sprigs, lemon wedges and avocado slices. Great for lunch on Christmas Day! Serves 4.

ASPIC SALAD

2 packages Knox gelatin
2 tablespoons lemon juice
3½ cups V-8 juice
2 tablespoons fresh onion,
  grated

½ teaspoon Tabasco
4 ribs chopped celery
⅓ cup chopped green olives
2 large avocados, cut in small
  pieces

Soften gelatin in vinegar, lemon juice and 1½ cups V-8. Bring to a boil. Add remaining 2 cups V-8, onions, Tabasco, celery, olives and avocados. Congeal in 3-quart Pyrex dish and cut in squares to serve. Serves 12.

ZESTY BROCCOLI SPEARS

2 pounds fresh broccoli florets

Dressing:

1 cup orange juice	⅛ teaspoon garlic powder
2 tablespoons grated orange rind	3 tablespoons white wine vinegar
2 teaspoons lemon juice	2 tablespoons olive oil
¼ teaspoon garlic salt	

Trim off flower tops of broccoli and remove tough ends of lower stalks. Wash broccoli thoroughly, and cut into small spears. Cook broccoli in a small amount of boiling water 6-8 minutes, or just until tender. Drain. Place in a serving dish. Combine orange juice, rind, lemon juice, garlic salt and garlic powder in a small saucepan; stir well. Cover and cook over low heat for 10 minutes. Remove from heat, stir in vinegar and oil with a wire whisk. Pour mixture over broccoli. Serve as a hot or cold vegetable, or as a salad on a lettuce leaf. Serves 8.

BROCCOLI SALAD

2 pounds fresh broccoli (florets only)	1 cup raisins
2 cups carrots, thinly sliced	1 cup sunflower seeds, toasted
½ cup red onion, chopped	

Sauce:

1 cup mayonnaise	fresh ground pepper
¼ cup sugar	1 cup cooked bacon, crumbled
2 tablespoons apple cider vinegar	

Toss broccoli, onion, raisins, carrots and sunflower seeds. Mix next 4 ingredients for the sauce and add to the vegetable mixture. Marinate overnight in refrigerator. When you are ready to serve, add crumbled bacon and stir mixture well to distribute sauce evenly. Serves 8.

SPINACH SALAD WITH CITRUS DRESSING

1 pound spinach
1 carrot, grated
¼ cup shredded Cheddar cheese

2 slices bacon, cooked and
crumbled

Dressing:
⅓ cup juice from small
grapefruit
¾ teaspoon sugar
¼ teaspoon salt
¼ teaspoon pepper
¼ teaspoon dry mustard

¼ teaspoon dill weed
¼ teaspoon parsley
¼ teaspoon onion powder
¼ teaspoon dried basil
¼ cup vegetable oil
¼ cup vinegar

Combine dressing ingredients in a jar. Cover, shake and chill. Tear spinach into bite size pieces, and combine with grated carrot. Sprinkle with crumbled bacon and cheese. Serve with dressing. Variation: Add 1 hard boiled egg, chopped, and sliced mushrooms. Serves 4-6.

CHRISTMAS ELEGANT GREEN SALAD

2 Ruby Red grapefruit,
sectioned
4 cups fresh spinach, torn
1 head red-tipped lettuce,
torn

1 pint fresh strawberries,
halved
2 unpeeled red apples, sliced
½ pint fresh raspberries (if
available)

Peel and section grapefruit over bowl, reserving juice for dressing. Combine grapefruit, strawberries and apples with greens. Toss gently with **Ruby Poppyseed Dressing:** ¼ cup raspberry vinegar, ¼ cup grapefruit juice, 1 cup salad oil, ½ cup sugar, ½ teaspoon dry mustard, and 2 tablespoons poppyseeds. Mix well and pour over salad. Beautiful! 6-8 servings.

CORN SALSA RELISH

2 15-ounce cans corn,
drained
1 15-ounce can black beans,
drained and rinsed
½ cup picante sauce

1 cup red pepper, chopped
½ cup fresh cilantro, chopped
juice of 1 lime
salt, pepper and garlic
powder to taste

Mix all ingredients and chill. Colorful and pretty served in a glass bowl. Serves 6.

SALAD OF TART GREENS

1 medium red onion, sliced into thin rings
½ cup red wine vinegar
1 small head each: romaine, radicchio, red leaf lettuce and chicory
½ cup (4 ounces) pine nuts, toasted lightly (reserve 3 tablespoons)
3 to 4 whole scallions, thinly sliced on the diagonal (reserve one)

Dressing:
8 large cloves garlic, cut in ¼-inch pieces
½ cup olive oil
3 tablespoons red wine vinegar

3 ounces Parmigiano/Reggiano cheese, in thin curls (reserve half)
3 ounces thinly sliced prosciutto, cut in bite size portions (reserve half)
1 cup lightly packed fresh basil leaves
1 cup lightly packed Italian parsley leaves

3 tablespoons balsamic vinegar
1 tablespoon dark brown sugar
salt and pepper to taste

Clean greens and tear into bite-size pieces. Soak onion in ½ cup vinegar for about 30 minutes to cut its sharpness. Drain. Toss greens with all but 3 tablespoons of pine nuts, most of the scallions, half the cheese and prosciutto and all the basil and parsley. Arrange on large platter. The dressing: Slowly cook garlic in olive oil in a medium skillet over low heat about 5 minutes or until color barely changes. Remove with slotted spoon and reserve. Turn heat to medium high and add vinegars to oil, being cautious of hot splashes. Cook for a few minutes, or until the acid has diffused slightly. Add brown sugar and let mixture bubble slowly for about one minute. Taste for sweet-tart balance and add extra brown sugar or balsamic vinegar to taste. If dressing is too sharp, simmer a few minutes to cook off some of the vinegar's acid. Stir in reserved garlic and season with salt and pepper. Set aside to cool. Top salad with drained red onion and remainder of scallions, pine nuts, cheese and prosciutto. Reheat dressing to warm, stirring to blend. Spoon over salad and serve immediately. Generously serves 6-8 as an antipasto.

GREEK SALAD

5 medium tomatoes
2 medium cucumbers
1 small red onion

1 8-ounce package feta
  cheese
18 Calamata olives

Dressing:
4 tablespoons olive oil
3 tablespoons red wine
  vinegar

1 teaspoon salt
½ teaspoon pepper

Cut each tomato into 8 pieces. Peel, seed and cut cucumbers into chunks. Cut red onion into slices and separate into rings. Crumble feta cheese. Add olives. Place all of above ingredients into a bowl. Mix dressing and toss with salad. The ingredients can be prepared ahead, but should not be tossed with dressing until just before serving. Serves 6.

SALADE NIÇOISE

6 medium potatoes, peeled,
  boiled and sliced
1 small red onion, sliced into
  rings
3 ripe tomatoes, cut into
  sixths
2 cans white tuna, broken
  into chunks

12 anchovy fillets
6 hard-cooked eggs,
  quartered
green pepper rings
18 Calamata olives
romaine or red-tipped lettuce

Dressing:
¾ cup olive oil
½ cup wine vinegar
3 tablespoons fresh parsley,
  chopped, or 1 teaspoon
  dried

¼ teaspoon dried basil
1 teaspoon salt
½ teaspoon pepper

Toss potatoes and onions with ½ of dressing. Arrange lettuce on 6 plates. Divide potatoes and onion mixture with dressing among 6 plates. Then divide the tomatoes, tuna, anchovy fillets, hard-cooked eggs, olives and green pepper rings and put on each plate. Drizzle each plate with a little of the remainder of the dressing. Serve immediately. Serves 6.

HAM SALAD

2 tablespoons unflavored
    gelatin
½ cup cold water
1 cup hot tomato juice
1 tablespoon onion juice
1 tablespoon vinegar

¼ teaspoon salt
¼ teaspoon paprika
1 cup mayonnaise
2 cups ground ham
½ cup green onion, chopped
½ cup celery, chopped

Dissolve gelatin in water. Stir in tomato juice. Add onion, juice, vinegar, salt and paprika. Mix well and cool. When mixture begins to thicken, add mayonnaise, ham, green onion and celery. Put into lightly-mayonnaised loaf pan or Pyrex pan. Refrigerate until firm. Slice or cut into squares. Serves 8-12.

PICKLED BLACK-EYED PEAS

2 1-pound cans black eyed
    peas, drained
½ to 1 bunch green onions,
    chopped
½ cup safflower oil
¼ cup red wine vinegar
½ teaspoon garlic powder

1 tablespoon Worcestershire
    sauce
1 teaspoon salt
1 bay leaf
pepper to taste
1 or 2 dashes of Tabasco

Place peas and onions in a heat proof bowl. Bring to a boil all other ingredients in a saucepan and pour over peas. Refrigerate overnight or for several days. Great for New Year's day or for a delicious summer treat. Can be used as an hors d'oeuvre on crackers. Serves 8.

GREAT SALAD

use as many different greens
    as desired: Boston, green
    leaf, red leaf, radicchio,
    arugula, spinach, etc.

almonds, slivered and toasted
black and green olives, sliced
feta cheese, crumbled

Dressing:
⅔ cup olive oil
⅓ cup balsamic vinegar
3 tablespoons Dijon mustard

1 tablespoon shallots (or
    garlic), chopped
salt and pepper to taste

Toss ingredients with dressing. The amount of almonds, olives and feta cheese will vary according to the amount of greens used. Add more or less accordingly.

VEGETABLE MEDLEY SALAD

2 cans green beans, drained
1 can Mexican corn, drained
1 can artichokes, drained and
   sliced
1 4-ounce can sliced
   mushrooms, drained
1 cucumber, sliced thinly

2 green onions, chopped
   (include tops)
1 can sliced tomatoes,
   drained
coarse pepper
garlic salt

Dressing:
⅓ cup brown sugar
⅔ cup tarragon vinegar

½ cup salad oil
2 dashes Tabasco

Layer vegetables in a large bowl. Sprinkle layers with a little garlic salt and coarsely ground pepper as you layer it. Pour dressing over the salad. Refrigerate and let marinate for 12 to 24 hours. Serves 12.

SPINACH SALAD WITH HONEY DRESSING

¾ pound fresh spinach, torn
1 8-ounce can mandarin
   oranges, drained

¾ cup coarsely chopped
   walnuts, toasted

Dressing:
¼ teaspoon salt
1 clove garlic, crushed
⅓ cup honey

⅓ cup light olive oil
1 tablespoon lemon juice

Sprinkle salt in a salad bowl. Rub garlic into salt using the back of a wooden spoon. Add honey, oil and lemon juice. Beat with a wire whisk and refrigerate. When ready to serve, add spinach and remaining ingredients to dressing. Toss gently and serve immediately. Serves 4-6.

HOT SHRIMP SALAD

1 pound cooked small shrimp
¾ cup sliced canned water
    chestnuts
1¼ cups celery, thinly sliced
2 hard boiled eggs, chopped
    coarsely
3 tablespoons onion, grated

¾ cup mayonnaise
2 tablespoons lemon juice
½ teaspoon salt
¾ cup Cheddar cheese,
    shredded
1 cup potato chips, crushed

Combine shrimp, water chestnuts, celery, eggs and onion. Mix mayonnaise, lemon juice and salt. Stir in shrimp mixture. Place in greased 8- or 9-inch baking dish. Top with cheese and sprinkle potato chips on top. Bake at 325 or 350 degrees for 20 minutes. Note: This could be made with chicken rather than shrimp, by substituting one pound of cooked, cubed chicken breast. Serves 4-6.

COLD PASTA AND CHICKEN SALAD

8 ounces vermicelli pasta
1 cup garlic vinaigrette
    dressing (La Martinique
    Famous French dressing,
    if available)
10 fresh mushrooms, sliced
1 cup broccoli florets,
    blanched

10 cherry tomatoes, halved
    (optional)
2 cups cooked chicken
    breasts, sliced
⅓ cup fresh basil, chopped
    (or 1½ teaspoons dried)
⅓ cup toasted pine nuts

Cook pasta in boiling water. Drain well and place in mixing bowl. Add ⅓ cup dressing, toss, let cool and chill at least 3 hours. Place remaining dressing in another bowl. Add mushrooms, broccoli and tomatoes. Stir to coat thoroughly and chill. When ready to serve, add chicken to the pasta and toss. Add vegetables to chicken/pasta mixture. Add basil and pine nuts. Toss once more. Chill and serve. Serves 6.

CURRIED CHICKEN SALAD

6 whole chicken breasts,
  cooked and chopped
2 cups celery, chopped
¼ cup green onions, sliced
  thinly
2 cups mayonnaise
1 tablespoon curry powder
2 tablespoons chutney,
  chopped

2 6-ounce cans water
  chestnuts, drained and
  sliced
1 tablespoon soy sauce
1 unpeeled red or green
  apple, diced
1 pound grapes, green or red
2 tablespoons lemon juice
1 cup slivered almonds,
  toasted

Combine all ingredients except almonds and chill overnight. Sprinkle toasted almonds on top of chicken salad just before serving. Serves 8-10.

LEPRECHAUN SALAD
(FRUIT SALAD WITH HONEY LIME DRESSING)

4 kiwi fruit, peeled and sliced
2 red delicious apples,
  unpeeled, cored and
  sliced
2 pears, unpeeled, cored and
  sliced
½ cup seedless green grapes

½ cup seedless red grapes
lettuce leaves
1 2-ounce package slivered
  almonds, toasted
lime rind and strawberries for
  garnish

Dressing:
1 16-ounce carton plain
  yogurt

2 tablespoons honey
2 teaspoons grated lime rind

Prepare dressing by combining all ingredients. Arrange fruit on lettuce leaves and drizzle with dressing. Sprinkle with almonds and garnish, if desired. Serves 4.

CHICKEN SALAD WITH
RADICCHIO AND RED ONIONS

2 whole chicken breasts
½ cup all purpose flour
2 eggs
salt and freshly ground
    pepper
½ cup freshly grated
    Parmesan or Romano
    cheese
1 cup sesame (or safflower)
    oil

1 small head radicchio, thinly
    sliced lengthwise
1 small bunch arugula (we
    substitute red leafy
    lettuce separated into
    leaves)
1 red Spanish onion, thinly
    sliced

Dressing:
½ cup olive oil
¼ cup balsamic vinegar

2 tablespoons fresh lemon
    juice

Halve, skin and bone the chicken breasts. Trim off any excess fat. Place the breasts between 2 sheets of waxed paper, and using a rolling pin, flatten until the meat is of an even thickness, about ¼ inch. Lightly dust each breast with flour and shake off the excess. In a bowl beat together the eggs, salt and pepper. Dip the chicken pieces into the egg mixture to coat both sides thoroughly. Then dip into the cheese to coat. Warm the oil in a heavy frying pan over medium heat. When the oil is hot, add 2 breast halves and cook, turning as they become golden brown, 2 to 3 minutes per side. Transfer to paper towels to drain. Repeat with the remaining chicken. In a large bowl combine the radicchio, arugula and onion, reserving a few onion slices for garnish. In a small bowl whisk together the olive oil, vinegar and lemon juice; season to taste with salt and pepper. Pour over the salad greens and toss well. Slice each chicken breast lengthwise into thin strips. Place the salad greens on a large serving plate. Top with the chicken strips and remaining onion slices. Serves 4.

GRILLED STEAK SALAD ANTIPASTO

2 heads Boston (or Bibb)
lettuce, torn into bite size
pieces

2 red peppers, roasted, peeled
and cut into 1-inch
strips, or use a 7-ounce
jar of roasted peppers

1 14-ounce can hearts of
palm, drained, rinsed and
cut diagonally into
½-inch thick slices

1 6-ounce jar marinated
artichoke hearts, drained
and halved

¼ pound fresh mushrooms,
thinly sliced

½ cup herbed vinaigrette, or
bottled dressing

2 teaspoons Dijon mustard

1½ pounds beef top round
steak, about 1 inch thick

salt and pepper to taste

In a large bowl, toss together first five ingredients. Arrange on large serving platter or individual plates. In a small bowl, whisk together vinaigrette and mustard. Prepare grill for cooking. Place steak on grill and cook for about 20 minutes for rare, turning once (if oven-broiling, place steak on rack 3-5 inches from heat source. Broil 20 minutes for rare, turning once). Remove from grill; let rest for 10-15 minutes before slicing into ½-inch thick slices. Sprinkle with salt and pepper to taste. Arrange steak slices on top of salad; drizzle with dressing. Advance preparation: If grilling over the weekend, throw an extra steak on the grill for this salad. Chill steak for a head start on a quick-to-make weekday meal. Cooked meat will keep 2-3 days in the refrigerator. Delicious served warm or chilled. Serves 6.

MELON PICO DE GALLO

½ cup fresh lemon juice

½ cup fresh cilantro leaves,
chopped

¼ cup honey

2 teaspoons fresh jalapeños,
seeded and finely minced

2 cups jícama, diced

2 cups cantaloupe, diced

8 cups watermelon, seeded
and diced

Whisk lemon juice, cilantro, honey and jalapeño to blend. Refrigerate for 2 hours. Pour over remaining ingredients, toss and serve in a hollowed-out watermelon half. Serves 50.

MOM'S FESTIVE RED APPLE CHRISTMAS SALAD

6 Granny Smith apples
1 cup sugar
½ cup water

1 package cinnamon candy
(red hots)
2 or 3 drops red food coloring

Stuffing:
1 4-ounce package cream
    cheese
¼ to ½ cup finely chopped
    toasted pecans

¼ cup powdered sugar
2 tablespoons milk

Peel and core apples. In saucepan, boil sugar, water and candy until all the candy melts, stirring constantly. Add red food coloring to liquid. Drop peeled, cored apples into hot, boiling sugar water and cook until tender. Ladle to a Pyrex dish to cool.

Pour extra syrup over apples to glaze as they cool. Mix stuffing to desired consistency. Spoon stuffing into center of each cooled apple. Refrigerate. Arrange on lettuce leaf to serve. Serves 6.

MERRY BERRY SALAD

1 6-ounce package raspberry
    gelatin
1½ cups boiling water
1 10-ounce package frozen
    raspberries, thawed (do
    not drain)
1 teaspoon lemon juice
1 pint sour cream

1 6-ounce package cherry
    gelatin
½ cup boiling water
1 15-ounce can crushed
    pineapple (do not drain)
1 16-ounce can Ocean Spray
    whole berry cranberry
    sauce

First layer: Dissolve raspberry gelatin in boiling water. Add raspberries and the liquid. Add lemon juice. Stir well and pour into a 13 x 9-inch Pyrex dish. Refrigerate until firm. Second layer: Spread sour cream over the first layer with a spatula. Refrigerate, uncovered, for about one hour. Third layer: As soon as you place the second layer on the first and put it back into the refrigerator, begin making the third layer. Dissolve cherry gelatin in the water. Add pineapple and cranberry sauce and mix well. Chill until slightly thickened. Using a gravy ladle, carefully spoon this mixture over the second layer. As soon as it has congealed, carefully cover with plastic wrap so that it will not dry out. Try to stretch the wrap so that it does not touch the salad.

MANGO MOUSSE

3 small packages jello (3
  lemon or 2 lemon and 1
  orange)
2½ cups boiling water

1 large jar mangoes with
  juice (found in produce
  department)
8 ounces cream cheese
¼ cup lemon juice (or more to
  taste)

Dissolve gelatin in boiling water. Blend other ingredients in
blender, and then mix with gelatin. Chill in 9 x 13-inch pan for 24
hours. This salad can be cut with a biscuit cutter or other shape
for interest. Serve on a bed of lettuce.

FESTIVE CRANBERRIES

1 cup sugar
½ cup orange juice
2 cups cranberries
¼ cup chopped, seeded,
  peeled orange

1 tablespoon grated orange
  peel
¼ cup orange flavored
  liqueur (Grand Marnier)

Heat sugar and orange juice in large saucepan, stirring occasionally until sugar dissolves, 3 to 4 minutes. Stir in cranberries,
orange and peel. Heat to boiling, then reduce heat. Simmer uncovered until juice is released from cranberries, about 10
minutes. Add liqueur and simmer 2 minutes. Refrigerate covered,
overnight. This is also great with ½ cup chopped toasted pecans
or walnuts. Serves 8.

PINEAPPLE-CRANBERRY SALAD

1 pound fresh cranberries
1 orange, peeled and seeded
2 cups sugar
2 cups pineapple juice
4 tablespoons unflavored
  gelatin

¾ teaspoon salt
3 stalks celery, medium
  chopped
1 cup toasted pecans,
  chopped
5 slices pineapple, diced

Process cranberries and orange in food processor. Add sugar and
let stand one hour. Bring pineapple juice to boil and dissolve
gelatin in it. Combine with cranberry mixture and add salt, celery,
pecans and pineapple. Pour into an oiled 9 x 13-inch casserole or
large oiled mold and chill. Cut in squares and serve on a curly
lettuce leaf.

MUSTARD VINAIGRETTE DRESSING

1 tablespoon Dijon mustard
3 tablespoons white wine
  (or tarragon vinegar)
1 teaspoon dried tarragon
  (or 1 tablespoon fresh)

½ teaspoon salt
½ teaspoon freshly ground
  black pepper
¾ cup extra virgin olive oil

Place mustard in a small bowl. Add vinegar, tarragon, salt and pepper, and whisk well. Slowly drizzle in olive oil, whisking constantly until dressing is creamy. Yields 1 cup.

BLEU CHEESE DRESSING

1 cup mayonnaise
1 cup sour cream
¾ to 1 cup buttermilk
2 tablespoons dill pickle juice

1 tablespoon Worcestershire
  sauce
1 teaspoon garlic powder
2 to 4 ounces bleu cheese,
  crumbled

Mix all ingredients together and allow to stand for blending of flavors (20 minutes). Adjust to taste the mayonnaise, sour cream or buttermilk. Yields 3½ cups.

BEST SALAD DRESSING

½ cup sugar
½ teaspoon paprika
¼ teaspoon dry mustard
½ teaspoon salt
½ teaspoon Worcestershire
  sauce

½ teaspoon onion, grated
1 cup olive oil (or canola oil)
½ cup vinegar (flavored or
  balsamic)
¼ cup sesame seed, toasted
  (optional)

Combine all ingredients and whisk vigorously to mix. Store in a covered jar in refrigerator. Shake well before using. Delicious on mixed greens or spinach, toasted walnuts, goat cheese and mandarin oranges. Yields 2 cups.

ARTICHOKE MAYONNAISE

2 shallots
1 can artichokes, well drained
2 large egg yolks
2 tablespoons lemon juice
1 teaspoon Dijon mustard

2 teaspoons fresh dill (or 1
   teaspoon dried)
½ teaspoon Tabasco
½ teaspoon salt
dash of pepper
1⅓ cups salad oil

Snip 2 shallots with scissors into fine pieces. Use white blade of food processor. Add one ingredient at a time with the machine running: artichoke, egg yolks, lemon juice, Dijon mustard, fresh dill, Tabasco, salt, and pepper. Slowly add 1⅓ cups salad oil (add 2 tablespoons first and mix well - then slowly add rest through tube). Great as a dip for veggies, delicious on sliced tomatoes, or on baked potatoes. Yields 1½ pints.

> *For every teaspoon of dried herbs, the equivalent is 3 teaspoons of fresh herbs — a three to one ratio.*

WHITE HOUSE DRESSING

4 shallots, finely minced
1 garlic clove, finely minced
1 tablespoon Worcestershire
   sauce
1 teaspoon salt
⅛ teaspoon freshly ground
   black pepper

juice of one lemon
1½ tablespoons Dijon
   mustard
½ cup red wine vinegar
1 cup olive or vegetable oil

Whisk and serve over salad greens.

ZERO CALORIE SALAD DRESSING

1 cup tomato juice or V-8
   juice
4 tablespoons lemon juice or
   vinegar

2 tablespoons onion, grated
Mrs. Dash to taste
dash of Worcestershire sauce

Place in a jar with a lid. Shake and serve over garden salad. Yields 1 cup.

CREAMY CAESAR SALAD DRESSING

½ cup mayonnaise
⅓ cup red wine vinegar
¼ teaspoon Tabasco
½ teaspoon salt

¼ teaspoon pepper
2 large cloves garlic
3 ounces grated Parmesan
   cheese

Put mayonnaise, vinegar, Tabasco, salt and pepper into a bowl. Either press or mince garlic finely and add to the bowl. Add grated Parmesan cheese and mix well. Can be kept in the refrigerator until needed. Yields 1 cup.

GRAPEFRUIT (OR ORANGE) RASPBERRY VINAIGRETTE

3 tablespoons grapefruit juice
   (or orange juice)
1 tablespoon raspberry
   vinegar
¼ cup light olive oil

salt and freshly ground
   pepper, to taste
2 teaspoons tarragon,
   chopped

Mix grapefruit juice and vinegar together in a small bowl. Slowly add oil, whisking until smooth. Season with salt and pepper, stir in tarragon. Makes ½ cup.

Sauces

Palestine Hot Pepper Festival

Small, savory, spicy – HOT PEPPERS!
Aromatic and delicious hot peppers
enliven just about any food. Likewise,
Palestine is also uniquely seasoned. It
abounds in cultural diversity, historic
Victorian houses and breathtaking
dogwood trails.

Annually Palestine salutes the hot pepper
in late October. Parades, antique cars, a
pepper-eating contest, Tour de Pepper
Bicycle Ride and a volleyball tournament
provide a ZESTFUL time relished by all!

A center of railroading since 1873,
Palestine attracted a culturally divergent
population. Early businesses were begun
by German bakers, Norwegian jewelers,
and Czech tailors, and descendants
are still operating those family
enterprises today.

BASIC BEEF BROTH

1 to 2 pounds marrow bones
1 pound lean beef, cubed
leftover beef bones (the more
    the better)
3 sprigs parsley
1 carrot, chopped

1 small onion, chopped
1 tomato (or 1 tablespoon
    tomato paste)
salt and pepper to taste
1 clove garlic (optional)
1 stalk celery with leaves

Place meat and bones in a shallow pan and roast at 450 degrees for 30 minutes. Prepare vegetables and place in a large kettle. Add bones, meat, salt and pepper. Add cold water to cover. Simmer, covered, for 3 hours. Skim off froth as necessary. Strain broth through colander. Cool. Remove any solidified fat. Can be further reduced to intensify flavors. Note: This stock is far less salty and more delicate in flavor than commercial products. Can be frozen in small quantities, such as in ice cube trays, then stored in freezer bags to be used later. Yields 3 quarts.

BROWN SAUCE

2 tablespoons shortening
1/3 cup flour
1 1/2 cups beef broth
3 teaspoons tomato paste

1/8 teaspoon pepper
1/2 cup beef broth, simmered
    to reduce by 1/2

Melt shortening in a heavy pan over low heat. Stir in flour and cook, stirring frequently, until this roux turns brown. Add broth and stir. Add tomato paste and let come to a boil. Add pepper and simmer over very low heat for about 2 hours, stirring frequently. The sauce should not be too thick. Add more broth to thin if necessary. Skim off fat. Add reduced beef broth. Strain, cool and keep covered in refrigerator. Keeps 2 weeks. Can be frozen. Yields 1 1/2 cups.

SAUCE VELOUTÉ

¼ cup butter or margarine
⅓ cup flour
1½ cup chicken broth (less if juices of the dish are being added)

salt and pepper to taste
nutmeg to taste
1 egg yolk
⅓ cup cream or milk

Make a white roux by melting butter in a heavy pan over low heat, then blending in the flour. Do not brown. Pour in the hot broth and stir until well blended. Add seasoning to taste and cook 45 minutes to 1 hour over hot water or very low heat. May be refrigerated for several days, or frozen. When ready to use, add egg yolk beaten with a little of the sauce. Do not boil after adding the egg yolk. Delicious when served with poultry, lamb, veal, fish, eggs and vegetables. White sauces such as this and Béchamel tend to thicken as they cook and may need thinning to keep them from becoming too stiff or heavy. For this sauce, use broth as thinner. See Sauce Béchamel. Yields 2 cups.

SAUCE BÉCHAMEL

¼ cup butter or margarine
⅓ cup flour
1½ cup hot milk
salt and pepper to taste

nutmeg to taste
1 egg yolk
⅓ cup cream or milk

This sauce is prepared the same way as Sauce Velouté, except hot milk has been substituted for the meat broth. Serve with poultry, lamb, veal, fish, eggs, and vegetables such as broccoli, cauliflower, asparagus and spinach. White sauces such as this and Sauce Velouté tend to thicken as they cook and may need thinning to keep them from becoming too stiff or heavy. For this sauce, use milk as thinner. Variation on Béchamel: Sauce Aurore uses 1½ cups sauce with 1 tablespoon tomato paste and one egg. See Sauce Velouté. Yields 2 cups.

BASIC OVEN-DRIED TOMATOES

28 medium plum tomatoes
(about 4 pounds)
2½ teaspoons extra virgin
olive oil

1 teaspoon salt
fresh ground pepper to taste

Preheat oven to 200 degrees. Core and cut off ends of tomatoes, then halve lengthwise. Using pastry brush, lightly coat the skin side of each tomato half with olive oil. Place skin side down on large baking sheet. Sprinkle with salt and pepper to taste. Bake until they shrink to about ¼ of original size, 4 to 6 hours (they should remain soft and juicy). Let cool on baking sheet. Place in container and refrigerate. Variations: 1. Follow basic recipe but sprinkle with thyme or basil, or your favorite seasoning. 2. Rosemary orange variation is made by substituting 1 tablespoon rosemary oil and ½ teaspoon orange oil instead of the olive oil. Yields 2 cups.

OVEN-DRIED TOMATO PESTO

1 cup oven-dried tomatoes
4 tablespoons slivered
almonds, toasted
2 tablespoons bread crumbs
4 medium garlic cloves,
peeled and chopped
coarsely

½ teaspoon lemon zest
2 tablespoons olive oil
½ cup tomato juice
½ teaspoon salt
pepper to taste

Place tomatoes, almonds, bread crumbs, garlic, lemon zest, olive oil and tomato juice in blender or food processor. Process until smooth. Add salt and pepper. Process to blend. Serve on pasta, veal or chicken. Wonderful on cold pasta, penne or other of your choice. Yields 2 cups.

CHILI SAUCE

12 large tomatoes
3 large onions
3 large peppers
1 cup brown sugar
1 cup vinegar
1 teaspoon cloves, ground

1 teaspoon nutmeg
1 teaspoon cinnamon
1 teaspoon ginger
1 teaspoon celery seed
salt and pepper to taste

Chop vegetables and place in large pot. Cook uncovered slowly about 3 hours. Do not add sugar and spices until nearly done to avoid turning dark. Yields 3½ pints.

CLAM SAUCE

9 tablespoons olive oil
6 medium-large garlic cloves, chopped
3 10½-ounce cans baby clams, drained
6 tablespoons fresh parsley, chopped

1¼ cups clam juice
2 tablespoons dried oregano
2 tablespoons dried basil
¾ teaspoon salt
¾ teaspoon pepper
½ teaspoon crushed red pepper flakes (optional)

In a large skillet heat oil on medium heat. Add garlic and sauté until golden, 3 to 4 minutes. Add clams and parsley and sauté 1 minute more. Add remaining ingredients and gently simmer about 3 minutes before pouring over hot pasta. Can be made ahead and reheated. Yields 4-6 servings.

DILL SAUCE

1 cup mayonnaise
1 cup sour cream
½ teaspoon salt
¼ teaspoon pepper
¼ teaspoon Tabasco

2 teaspoons dried dill
2 tablespoons snipped chives
¼ teaspoon white pepper
¾ cup coarsely chopped cucumber

Mix all ingredients and chill before serving. Serve with Salmon Mousse or salad of your choice.

PLUM SAUCE

1½ cups red plum jam
1½ teaspoons prepared
   mustard

1½ teaspoons horseradish
1½ teaspoons fresh lemon
   juice

Combine all ingredients in small saucepan, mixing well. Place over low heat just until warm, stirring constantly. Use with ham or pork. Yields 1¾ cups.

PUTTANESCA SAUCE

¼ cup olive oil
1 cup black olives, pitted and
   halved
½ cup sun-dried tomatoes,
   cut in ¼-inch strips
½ cup capers
8 cloves garlic, chopped

6 anchovies, mashed
3 cups plum tomatoes,
   peeled, seeded and
   quartered
¼ cup fresh basil or finely
   chopped Italian parsley

Place oil and first 5 ingredients in a saucepan and simmer until anchovies dissolve. Add plum tomatoes and basil or parsley. Simmer until tomatoes soften and break up. Serve over 1 pound cooked pasta. If desired, substitute for the dried tomatoes a 1-pound can of tomatoes, squeezed to remove juice and seeds. Garlic may also be cut by ½, if preferred. Yields 5½ cups.

RED SAUCE FOR PASTA

2 cloves garlic, sliced
2 to 3 tablespoons olive oil
½ medium yellow onion,
   chopped
½ cup finely chopped tomato

1 large can tomatoes, whole
   or chopped
1 tablespoon spaghetti sauce
   seasoning
1 tablespoon Italian herb
   seasoning

Sauté onion in olive oil until translucent. Add garlic and continue to sauté 1 to 2 minutes. Add tomatoes and seasonings. Simmer on low heat 45 minutes to 1 hour. Optional: Add 1½ cups browned Italian sausage or grilled chicken to sauce before spooning over pasta. Yields 3 cups.

PESTO SAUCE

2 garlic cloves
1 teaspoon salt
2 cups fresh basil, washed
    and dried
2 tablespoons pine nuts,
    finely chopped

½ cup olive oil
½ cup Parmesan cheese
2 tablespoons Romano cheese
4 tablespoons softened butter
2 tablespoons hot water

In a food processor place garlic, salt, basil, nuts and oil. Process. Add cheeses and 4 tablespoons softened butter. Process. When ready to serve, add 2 tablespoons water (from boiling the pasta). Serve at room temperature over linguini. If freezing this recipe, omit the water until ready to serve. Yields 1½ cups.

PICANTE SAUCE

12 large ripe tomatoes
    (peeled if desired)
2 cups jalapeño peppers, caps
    and seeds removed (1
    cup peppers may be used
    for milder sauce)

2 medium sweet onions, cut
    into chunks
1½ cups lemon juice or 2 cups
    vinegar
2 ribs celery, cut into chunks
    (optional)
2 tablespoons sugar

NOTE: WEAR RUBBER GLOVES TO PROTECT HANDS FROM HOT PEPPERS! Place ingredients in blender and process to a point where small pieces of pepper and onion remain. Simmer in heavy saucepan, stirring frequently, until desired thickness is attained. Pour boiling sauce into hot canning jars; wipe edge carefully. Seal one jar at a time and place in boiling water bath canner and process for 35 minutes. Makes approximately 3 pints.

FRESH TOMATO SAUCE

3 large tomatoes, seeded and
   diced
2 cloves garlic, chopped
1 small onion, chopped
10 large fresh basil leaves,
   chopped
1 tablespoon oregano,
   chopped

1 teaspoon rosemary
1 pound pasta, cooked
   according to package
   directions
salt to taste
juice of 1 lemon
½ cup olive oil

Put vegetables and herbs in large pasta bowl. Add 1 pound of cooked pasta and toss together. Add salt. Serve hot or at room temperature. Yields 2½ cups.

PRALINE SAUCE

1 cup brown sugar
¼ cup Karo syrup
2 tablespoons butter
½ cup half and half

1 teaspoon vanilla
⅛ teaspoon salt
1 cup pecans, toasted

Put brown sugar, Karo and butter in saucepan over low heat. Once this is melted, add half and half and remaining ingredients. Serve over baked brie with thin gingersnaps as a dessert. Also wonderful over ice cream.

BASIC WHITE SAUCE

¾ cup unsalted butter, melted
¾ cup all purpose flour

3 cups milk, heated

Over low heat, melt butter and stir in flour. Slowly pour in milk. Stir until thick. Yields 3 cups.

CAPER SAUCE

1½ cups Basic White Sauce
1 tablespoon capers

2 tablespoons white wine
   vinegar, or white wine

Add capers and vinegar (or wine) to Basic White Sauce. Serve with fish or lamb. Yields 2 cups.

MORNAY SAUCE

1½ cups Basic White Sauce   ½ cup white wine
¾ cup grated cheese

Add cheese and wine to Basic White Sauce. Serve with meat, fish or vegetables. Yields 2½ cups.

MUSTARD SAUCE

1½ cups Basic White Sauce   1 teaspoon dry mustard

Add mustard to Basic White Sauce. Serve with grilled fish. Yields 1½ cups.

RAVIGOTE SAUCE

1½ cups Basic White Sauce   1 tablespoon mustard
chervil to taste   1 chopped green onion (white
tarragon to taste   part only)
chives to taste

Add chervil, tarragon, chives, mustard and onion to Basic White Sauce. Serve cold with vegetables, meats and fish. Yields 1¾ cups.

HORSERADISH CREAM SAUCE

This is delicious with fillet of beef, smoked fish, or corned beef.

¾ cup whipping cream   2 tablespoons Dijon mustard
½ cup mayonnaise   freshly ground pepper and
½ cup prepared horseradish,   salt to taste
    drained   pinch of sugar

Whip cream in a bowl until it forms soft peaks. Combine the mayonnaise, horseradish, and mustard in another bowl. Using a spatula, fold in whipped cream. Add pepper, salt, and sugar to taste. Stir well.

SOS (SAVE ON SALT) SEASONING

1 teaspoon chili powder
2 teaspoons ground oregano
3 tablespoons paprika
3 tablespoons poultry
   seasoning

1 tablespoon garlic powder
6 tablespoons onion powder
2 tablespoons dry mustard
2 teaspoons black pepper

Combine all ingredients and mix well. Spoon into a shaker. Yields about 1 cup.

JOE'S BARBECUE SAUCE

2 10-ounce bottles
   Worcestershire sauce
2 10-ounce bottles Heinz 57
   sauce
2 10-ounce bottles A-1 sauce
1 can diced Rotel tomatoes
4 15-ounce cans tomato
   sauce or 2 28-ounce
   bottles catsup

1 small container Accent
1 heaping tablespoon garlic
   salt
1 heaping tablespoon onion
   salt
juice of 3 large lemons
¼ pound butter
½ pint honey
salt and pepper to taste

Mix ingredients in a large saucepan and simmer on top of stove for 2 hours. Stir frequently to prevent sticking. Use immediately or refrigerate for future use.

Seafood

Noonday Onion Festival

How sweet it is! This festival embodies the spirit of the county fair. Friends and family gather to share in the celebration honoring this succulent bulb.

The "Sweetest of the Sweet" contest singles out the tastiest onion of all, and the onion cook-off showcases a myriad of recipes – even an onion sundae!

Woodwork, arts and crafts, music, storytelling, and wonderful food culminate in a "fine time had by all!"

FRIED SCALLOPS WITH CITRUS GINGER SAUCE

¾ pound sea scallops, rinsed
    and drained well

¾ cup cornstarch
vegetable oil for frying

Sauce:

3 tablespoons fresh lemon
    juice
1½ tablespoons fresh orange
    juice

1½ tablespoons ginger root,
    freshly grated
1½ teaspoons cornstarch
1½ teaspoons sesame oil
½ teaspoon salt

To make sauce, in a small bowl stir together lemon juice, orange juice, ginger root, cornstarch, sesame oil and salt. Dredge scallops in cornstarch, coating them well and shaking off excess. Fry in ½ inch oil, preheated to 375 degrees, for 1 to 1½ minutes on each side until golden. Transfer with a slotted spoon to another skillet. Stir sauce and pour it over scallops. Bring liquid to a boil, stirring constantly. Simmer and stir for 30 seconds to 1 minute, or until sauce is thickened and scallops are heated through. Serves 2.

EASY SCAMPI

¼ cup onion, finely chopped
4 cloves garlic, crushed
4 sprigs parsley, chopped
¾ cup butter, melted
2 pounds fresh medium
    shrimp, peeled and
    deveined

¼ cup dry white wine
2 tablespoons lemon juice,
    freshly squeezed
salt and freshly ground
    pepper to taste

Sauté onion, garlic and parsley in butter until onion is tender. Reduce heat to low and add shrimp. Cook, stirring frequently, about 5 minutes. Remove shrimp with a slotted spoon to a serving dish; keep warm. Add remaining ingredients to butter mixture and simmer 2 minutes. Pour mixture over shrimp. Serve immediately with French bread and salad. Serves 4.

SPICY TEXAS SHRIMP

1 large onion, chopped
2 large garlic cloves, minced
2 tablespoons oil
2 large tomatoes, chopped
1 4-ounce can chopped
    chilies, drained

2 pounds medium shrimp,
    peeled and deveined
¼ cup lime juice
¼ cup chopped cilantro
½ teaspoon salt

In a large skillet, cook onion and garlic in oil until tender. Add tomatoes, chilies and shrimp. Cook until shrimp turn pink. Stir in lime juice, cilantro and salt. Serve shrimp mixture wrapped in warm flour tortillas with guacamole and sour cream if desired. Serves 4.

CURRIED SHRIMP

2 tablespoons onion, finely
    chopped
2 tablespoons butter or
    margarine
2 tablespoons green pepper,
    seeded and diced
1 tablespoon curry powder
    (more or less to taste)
¼ teaspoon powdered ginger

½ teaspoon salt
1 cup chicken stock
1 cup half and half (divided
    use)
2 tablespoons flour
1 tablespoon cornstarch
4 cups shrimp, cooked,
    shelled and deveined

Sauté onion in butter or margarine in a heavy saucepan until onion is transparent. Remove onion. Add green pepper and sauté until limp but not brown. Remove from pan. Add curry powder and ginger, and cook while stirring for 1 minute. Add the onion and green pepper, along with salt, chicken stock and ¾ cup cream. Heat to boiling. Blend flour and cornstarch with the other ¼ cup cream, and mix to a smooth paste. Add slowly to hot mixture, cooking over low heat and stirring until smooth and thickened. Add shrimp and correct seasoning if necessary. Serve hot over rice with condiments of choice, such as peanuts, chutney, raisins, coconut, etc. This can be kept hot in the top of a chafing dish. Serves 6-8.

SHRIMP ALA CREOLE

4 pounds shrimp, peeled and
  deveined
¾ cup oil
½ cup flour
1 bunch shallots, chopped, or
  1 large onion, chopped

1 small garlic, minced
salt and pepper to taste
1 6-ounce can tomato paste
4 green peppers, chopped
4 to 5 cups hot water
  (divided use)

Boil shrimp for 5 minutes. Drain immediately and rinse in cool water. Using iron skillet, make a roux with oil and flour. Brown well. Add onions and brown slightly. Add shrimp, salt and pepper. Stir until each shrimp is coated with the roux and none of the roux and onions stick to the skillet. Add tomato paste, green peppers and garlic. Stir for 15 minutes on LOW heat. After all tomato paste is sticking to the shrimp, pour 1 cup hot water in bottom of skillet and continue to cook on LOW. Let cook for 15 minutes more, stir well, and add, slowly, 3 to 4 cups hot water. If this method is used carefully, the rich gravy will cling to the shrimp, but if the ordinary stew method is used, the shrimp will appear naked, with no gravy sticking to them. HEAVEN FORBID. Taste to see if there is enough salt and pepper. Cook on LOW heat for 1 hour and serve over cooked rice. This is a delicious dish, and New Orleans is famous for it, but so often what is advertised as Shrimp Creole turns out to be only shrimp stew. Be sure to follow the recipe very carefully!

SPANISH RICE WITH SHRIMP

1 small onion, chopped
½ small green pepper,
   chopped
1 tablespoon butter
1 10½-ounce can beef broth
1 cup water
1 14½-ounce can stewed
   tomatoes in tomato juice

1 12-ounce jar picante salsa,
   mild
1 cup rice
1 4-ounce can chopped green
   chilies, drained
1 pound medium shrimp,
   shelled and deveined
1 10-ounce package frozen
   peas, thawed

In a 3-quart saucepan, sauté onion and green pepper in butter until crisp-tender, about 4 minutes. Add beef broth, water, stewed tomatoes, salsa and rice. Bring to a boil. Reduce heat, cover and simmer 20 minutes. Add chilies, uncooked shrimp and peas. Toss to mix well. Simmer another 5 minutes, or until rice is cooked and shrimp are pink and tender. Serves 4.

SHRIMP DE JONGHE
(BAKED SHRIMP IN GARLIC SAUCE)

½ pound (about 14) shrimp,
   shelled and deveined
3 tablespoons unsalted
   butter, softened
¼ teaspoon garlic, minced
   and mashed
1 tablespoon medium-dry
   sherry

⅓ cup fresh parsley leaves,
   minced
¼ cup fine dry bread crumbs
2 tablespoons sliced almonds,
   lightly toasted
lemon wedges as garnish

In a saucepan of boiling salted water, cook shrimp for 30 seconds. Drain in a colander, and run cold water over them. In a small bowl, cream together butter, garlic and sherry. Stir in parsley and bread crumbs. Salt and pepper to taste. Place shrimp, patted dry, into a buttered shallow baking dish just large enough to hold them tightly in one layer; dot with buttered mixture and top with almonds. Bake shrimp mixture in a preheated 400 degree oven, basting occasionally, for 15 minutes. Serve garnished with lemon. Serves 2.

SESAME SHRIMP AND ASPARAGUS

1 pound shrimp, peeled and
    deveined
1 pound asparagus
2 tablespoons sesame seeds
¼ cup salad oil

2 small onions, thinly sliced
1 tablespoon soy sauce
1 teaspoon salt
3 cups hot cooked rice

About 30 minutes before serving, prepare asparagus. Hold base of stalk firmly and bend stalk; end will break off at spot where it becomes too tough to eat. Discard ends. Trim scales if stalks are gritty. Cut into 2-inch pieces and set aside. In a large skillet or wok, over medium heat, toast sesame seeds until golden, stirring and shaking occasionally. Remove sesame seeds to a small bowl and set aside. In the same skillet or wok, over medium-high heat, add salad oil and cook shrimp, asparagus and onion, stirring quickly and frequently (stir fry), until shrimp are pink and vegetables are crisp-tender, about 5 minutes. Stir in sesame seeds, soy sauce and salt until mixed. Serve with rice. Serves 4.

SHRIMP DIJON

1½ pounds shrimp, fresh or
    frozen
7 tablespoons butter
2 teaspoons parsley, chopped
1 can pimento, chopped
1 teaspoon Worcestershire
    sauce

1½ tablespoons lemon juice,
    freshly squeezed
2 tablespoons flour
1 cup milk
1 cup Cheddar cheese,
    shredded
¼ teaspoon pepper
1 teaspoon dry mustard

Shell and devein shrimp. Melt ¼ cup butter in skillet. Add shrimp, parsley, pimento, Worcestershire sauce and lemon juice. Sauté 5 minutes. Melt remaining butter in saucepan. Add flour and stir until smooth. Gradually add milk, stirring. Add cheese, pepper and dry mustard. Cook over low heat until it thickens. Add shrimp mixture to cheese sauce and serve over rice. Serves 8.

SHRIMP-OKRA GUMBO

½ cup vegetable oil
½ cup all-purpose flour
2 cups fresh okra, chopped
1 cup celery, finely chopped
1½ cups onion, finely
    chopped
1 cup coarsely chopped green
    bell pepper
1 16-ounce can tomatoes

1 8-ounce can tomato sauce
2 10¾-ounce cans beef broth
2 cans water
2 pounds shrimp, peeled and
    deveined
1 cup fresh crab meat
    (optional)
1 pint oysters, drained
    (optional)

Seasonings:
4 cloves garlic, minced
1 teaspoon black pepper
2 teaspoons salt
3 bay leaves
1 teaspoon thyme

¼ teaspoon oregano
2 tablespoons sugar
1 teaspoon Tabasco
½ teaspoon cayenne pepper
1 tablespoon dry sherry

Make a roux by combining oil and flour in a large heavy pot. Be careful not to burn. Cook, stirring constantly over low to medium heat until mixture is deep brown. This will take about 30 minutes. Combine okra, celery, onions and peppers. Sauté in roux until tender. Add tomatoes, tomato sauce, broth, water and seasonings. Simmer 2 to 3 hours. Add seafood the last 20 minutes and simmer. Check for shrimp doneness. Remove from heat and serve over rice. Serves 8.

File powder is the spice of choice for gumbo. Sprinkle on to suit your taste as the gumbo is served over rice.

SEAFOOD ENCHILADAS

2 medium white onions,
  coarsely chopped
1 7-ounce can diced green
  chilies
1½ tablespoons butter
1 pound crab meat
1 pound tiny shrimp
1 cup walnut halves, toasted
1 12-ounce can medium
  pitted ripe olives,
  drained and halved
1 pound Monterey Jack
  cheese, shredded
1 pound Cheddar cheese,
  shredded
vegetable oil
12 corn tortillas
2 cups half and half
1 cup sour cream
½ cup butter, melted
1½ teaspoons dried oregano
1 teaspoon garlic salt
Cheddar cheese, shredded for
  garnish
sliced pimentos for garnish
avocado slices for garnish
sliced black olives for garnish

In a large skillet, sauté onions and chilies in butter until transparent. Remove from heat and add crab, shrimp, walnuts and olives. Combine cheeses. Set aside 1½ cups cheese for top of casserole. Stir remaining cheese into seafood mixture. In a skillet just large enough to hold tortillas, heat ¼ inch oil. Fry tortillas, one at a time, just long enough to soften, about 30 seconds. Drain on paper towels. Fill each tortilla with seafood filling, roll up and place, seam side down, in large, sprayed baking dish. This can be prepared in advance and refrigerated or frozen. Defrost before proceeding. In a medium saucepan, combine half and half, sour cream, butter, oregano and garlic salt. Stir frequently over medium heat until lukewarm and well blended. Pour over enchiladas. Sprinkle enchiladas with reserved cheese. Bake at 350 degrees for 30 minutes or until bubbly. Garnish with additional shredded cheese, pimento, avocados and olives. Simply sensational! Cooked and shredded chicken may be substituted for seafood. Serves 8.

PRIMER'S PICKLED SHRIMP

3 pounds shrimp, shelled, deveined and cooked in Shrimp Boil according to package directions

sliced onion for layering

Hot Marinade:
2 cups cider vinegar
1 cup lemon juice
1 cup salad oil
2 tablespoons sugar
6 whole bay leaves
1 teaspoon coarse ground pepper

1 teaspoon dill seed
½ teaspoon tarragon
1 teaspoon celery seed
1 teaspoon dry mustard
1 teaspoon salt
½ teaspoon cinnamon

Boil shelled shrimp 3 minutes in Shrimp Boil. Drain. Set aside. Mix and bring remaining ingredients to a boil, turn down heat and simmer for 10 minutes. Add shrimp and simmer 3 more minutes. Drain shrimp and layer in a large container with sliced onion. Cover with hot marinade and refrigerate at least 48 hours. Drain marinade and serve cold.

CAJUN SHRIMP AND PASTA

8 ounces angel hair pasta
8 ounces show peas
1 medium red pepper, cored and cut into thin strips
1 tablespoon diet margarine
1 large clove garlic, minced
1 tablespoon flour
2 cups white wine

¾ cup low sodium chicken broth (divided use)
½ teaspoon dried basil
½ teaspoon paprika
¼ teaspoon thyme
¼ teaspoon Tabasco
⅛ teaspoon black pepper
1 pound medium shrimp
1 tablespoon parsley

Cook pasta. Meanwhile, spray skillet with vegetable oil spray; heat on medium high. Add snow peas and bell pepper; cook 3 minutes. Remove and place in bowl. Add margarine to skillet; melt over medium heat. Add garlic and cook 1 minute. Sprinkle with flour. Cook 1 minute, stirring to blend. Gradually add wine and cook about 1 minute until smooth. Stir in ½ cup broth, basil, paprika, thyme, Tabasco and black pepper. Bring to boil. Add shrimp and reduce heat to medium low. Cook covered about 5 minutes. Return vegetables to skillet. Cook and stir 1 minute. Drain pasta and toss with ¼ cup broth. Add shrimp mixture to pasta and toss. Serves 6.

NEW ORLEANS SHRIMP

2 pounds raw shrimp
1 small peeled garlic
½ cup celery, finely chopped
1 green onion, finely chopped
chives to taste
6 tablespoons olive oil
3 tablespoons lemon juice
¼ teaspoon Tabasco

5 tablespoons horseradish
¼ teaspoon paprika
2 tablespoons prepared
    mustard
¾ teaspoon salt
½ teaspoon white pepper
avocado slices
shredded lettuce

Cook 2 pounds raw shrimp. Shell and devein. Rub a bowl with garlic. In same bowl, mix together celery, green onion, chives, olive oil, lemon juice, Tabasco, horseradish, paprika, mustard, salt and white pepper. If desired, marinate shrimp in sauce up to 12 hours. Refrigerate until ready to serve, or drizzle sauce over shrimp and avocado slices on a bed of shredded lettuce. Serves 4-6.

CRAB CAKES

1 tablespoon Creole mustard
1 tablespoon Worcestershire
    sauce
1 teaspoon seasoned salt
½ teaspoon pepper
½ teaspoon cayenne pepper
pinch of thyme
1 pound fresh crab meat,
    cartilage removed

1 cup Italian bread crumbs
    (or more)
2 teaspoons parsley, chopped
1 cup onion, finely chopped
⅓ cup mayonnaise
2 eggs, beaten
additional bread crumbs
olive oil
butter

Mix spices thoroughly. Add to mixture of crab meat, bread crumbs, parsley, onion and mayonnaise. Combine well and mold mixture into patties. Dip patties into beaten eggs, and then into additional bread crumbs. Sauté until crisp and brown in olive oil and butter. Serve plain and hot, or with a mayonnaise and white horseradish sauce. Serves 6.

CRAB ROLLS

1 pound crab meat (claw),
cartilage removed
2 large sweet onions,
chopped
3 cloves garlic, chopped
3 stalks celery, chopped
1 small bell pepper, chopped

6 fresh green onions,
chopped
½ cup parsley, chopped
1 cup bread crumbs
2 beaten eggs
salt and pepper to taste
cayenne pepper to taste

Sauté onions and garlic until limp; add chopped vegetables and cook briefly. Do not brown. Blend in remaining ingredients and cool. Shape into rolls. Roll in bread crumbs, then egg, and again in bread crumbs. Fry in hot oil until golden brown.

SEAFOOD CURRY

2 pounds fresh shrimp,
cleaned and cooked
1 7½-ounce can crab meat,
cartilage removed
6 tablespoons butter
6 tablespoons flour
1 8-ounce can cream of
coconut
3 cups milk
1 large onion, diced

1 teaspoon ground pepper
1 teaspoon salt
2 teaspoons paprika
5 tablespoons imported
Indian curry powder
(add enough water to
make paste)
1½ teaspoons powdered
ginger
1½ teaspoons domestic curry

In a large frying pan, melt butter over low heat. Add flour and stir. Add warmed cream of coconut and milk. Cook until thickened. Add onion, pepper, salt and paprika. Make a paste of imported curry and water, and add slowly TO TASTE. When desired flavor is reached, stir in ginger and domestic curry for sweetness. Mix in shrimp and crab meat. Simmer for 5 minutes. Let cool and refrigerate for at least 12 hours. When ready to use, reheat slowly for about 45 minutes at 325 degrees. Serve with rice and your choice of condiments, such as chutney, chopped onions, green peppers, peanuts, cashews, carrots, toasted coconut, raisins warmed in rum or chopped hard-boiled eggs. Serves 8-10.

GRILLED SALMON

8 4- to 6-ounce salmon fillets,
   1-inch thick
¼ cup butter, melted
2 tablespoons lemon juice
2 tablespoons fresh parsley,
   chopped

¼ teaspoon dill weed,
   rosemary, or marjoram,
   crushed
¼ teaspoon salt
⅛ teaspoon coarsely ground
   pepper

Combine all ingredients except salmon. Tear heavy-duty aluminum foil at least 2 inches longer than salmon; perforate with fork every 2 inches. Spray foil, and place salmon, skin-side down, on foil. Brush with butter mixture. Place cover on grill and form a tent over salmon with another piece of heavy-duty foil; seal edges. Barbecue over hot coals 5 minutes. Uncover and baste with butter mixture. Recover and barbecue 5 minutes longer or until salmon flakes easily when tested with fork (total time is 10 minutes per inch of thickness, measured at its thickest part). Baste with remaining butter mixture. Serves 8.

SALMON MOUSSE

1 8-ounce can tomato soup,
   undiluted
2 tablespoons unflavored
   gelatin (dissolved in ¼
   cup cold water)
1 large can red salmon,
   drained and flaked, or 1
   pound freshly poached
   salmon

1 cup mayonnaise (no
   cholesterol)
1 medium green pepper,
   finely chopped
½ teaspoon paprika
1 small sweet onion, grated
½ cup black olives, finely
   chopped
¼ teaspoon white pepper

Heat soup and cream cheese over low heat until cheese dissolves. Add softened gelatin and stir until well blended. Add remaining ingredients and mix well. Place in a well oiled fish mold, and chill overnight in refrigerator. Unmold on a bed of parsley or curly lettuce. Serve with Dill Sauce (see Sauces). Use a slice of olive for an eye. Serve as an appetizer or luncheon entrée with water crackers and grapes.

FISH IN A CHINESE GARDEN

2 pounds catfish fillets or
   shark steaks
2 tablespoons vegetable oil
1 cup green onion, chopped
1 cup celery, finely chopped
1 cup water chestnuts, sliced
   and drained

3 cups bean sprouts, fresh
1 cup snow peas, fresh
1 tablespoon lite soy sauce
dash white pepper
1 tablespoon cornstarch
2 tablespoons water

Prepare all vegetables in advance. Cut fish into bite-sized pieces. Heat vegetable oil in a large wok. Cook fish, stirring constantly with a wooden spoon. Do not brown fish. Remove fish pieces to a plate. Drain and reserve liquid. Add all vegetables to wok. Stir fry vegetables until they are just cooked and still crisp. Add reserved liquid, soy sauce and white pepper. Stir and add fish. Dissolve cornstarch in water and quickly add to fish and vegetables. When liquid thickens, serve over a bed of white rice. Serves 4-6.

GRILLED ORIENTAL FISH STEAKS

4 fish steaks, ⅝- to ¾-inch
   thick
¼ cup low sodium soy sauce
3 tablespoons minced onion

1 tablespoon fresh ginger
   root, grated
1 to 1½ tablespoons toasted
   sesame seed
½ teaspoon sesame oil

Place fish flat in a shallow dish. Mix next 5 ingredients well and pour over fish, allowing to marinate 15 to 20 minutes. Turn fish and spoon marinade evenly on opposite side. Marinate 15 minutes longer. Remove sesame seeds from fish before grilling. Grill over medium coals, approximately 10 minutes on each side, or until fish flakes when tested with fork. Serves 4.

RED SNAPPER À LA GEORGE

4 small snapper fillets
flour for dredging
3 tablespoons butter
salt and pepper to taste
½ cup fresh mushrooms,
  sliced

14 ounces canned artichoke
  hearts, drained and
  quartered
juice of 2 lemons
1 tablespoon Worcestershire
  sauce
water

Wash and dredge fillets in flour. Shake off excess. Melt butter in skillet and sauté fillets until well done on one side. Turn, lightly salt and pepper and cook well on second side. Cover fish with mushrooms and artichokes. Sprinkle with lemon juice and Worcestershire sauce.

Remove fish to serving platter. Add a bit of water to juice in skillet, heat, and pour over fish. Serve immediately. Serves 4.

FILLET OF SOLE STUFFED WITH SPINACH

4 fillets of sole
2 teaspoons lemon juice
1 10-ounce package chopped
  spinach, cooked and
  drained
¼ cup plus 2 tablespoons
  sour cream

2 tablespoons green onion,
  chopped
2 tablespoons parsley
⅛ teaspoon garlic powder
2 teaspoons dry bread
  crumbs
1 tablespoon margarine,
  melted

Mix drained spinach, sour cream, green onion, parsley and garlic powder together in a bowl. Sprinkle fillets with lemon juice. Place ¼ of spinach mixture in center of each fillet and roll up. Place fillets in shallow pan. Drizzle with margarine and sprinkle with bread crumbs. Bake at 350 degrees for 20-25 minutes, or until fish flakes with a fork. Serves 4.

GRILLED SWORDFISH STEAKS WITH SALSA

2 garlic cloves, minced
1½ teaspoons fresh oregano, finely chopped (or ½ teaspoon dried oregano)
1 teaspoon salt

2 tablespoons lime juice
⅓ cup olive oil
4 5- to 8-ounce swordfish steaks

Fresh Mexican Salsa:
1 fresh or canned serrano or jalapeño chilie
1 large tomato, seeded and finely chopped
2 green onions, chopped
½ garlic clove, minced
2 teaspoons olive oil

1 to 2 teaspoons finely chopped cilantro
½ to 1 teaspoon fresh lime juice
salt and freshly ground pepper to taste

Fresh Mexican Salsa: Wear plastic or rubber gloves to handle fresh chilie, and after handling, do not touch your face or eyes. Cut chilie open lengthwise, remove seeds and pith. Finely chop chilie. In a small bowl, combine chopped chilie, tomato, green onions, garlic, oil, cilantro and lime juice. Season with salt and pepper. Taste, and add more chilies, cilantro, lime juice, salt or pepper as needed. Makes about ¾ cup. Set aside Fresh Mexican Salsa. In a small bowl, combine garlic, oregano and salt. Beat in lime juice, then olive oil. Rinse fish steaks and wipe dry. Cover with lime marinade. Let stand at room temperature while preheating grill; oil the grill. Place 4 to 5 inches above hot coals. Turning once, grill 7 to 10 minutes or until fish tests done. Serve with Fresh Mexican Salsa. Serves 4.

PECAN ROUGHY WITH BROWN BUTTER SAUCE

6 6-ounce orange roughy fillets

Seasoning Mix for dredging (divided use)
½ cup milk
1 egg yolk

1 cup flour
vegetable oil
Brown Butter Sauce
Pecan Butter Sauce

Brown Butter Sauce:
1 cup chicken broth
1 teaspoon minced garlic
½ cup butter (divided)

2 tablespoons flour
¼ cup Worcestershire sauce
½ teaspoon Tabasco

Seasoning Mix:
2 tablespoons Greek seasoning
1 teaspoon onion powder
1 teaspoon paprika

1 teaspoon Creole seasoning
½ teaspoon red pepper
½ teaspoon white pepper

Pecan Butter Sauce:
½ cup butter, melted
1 cup pecans, chopped
2 tablespoons onions, chopped

1 clove garlic, minced
1 tablespoon lemon juice
1 teaspoon Tabasco

Seasoning Mix: Combine all ingredients in a small bowl, mixing well. **Brown Butter Sauce:** Combine broth and garlic in a small saucepan and bring to a boil. Reduce heat, and simmer 2 to 3 minutes. Melt ¼ cup butter in a heavy saucepan over low heat. Add flour, stirring until smooth. Cook 1 minute, stirring constantly. Gradually add broth mixture, stirring constantly. Add remaining ¼ cup butter, Worcestershire sauce and Tabasco. Cook over medium heat, stirring constantly, until mixture is thickened and bubbly hot. **Pecan Butter Sauce:** combine all ingredients in blender and set aside. To make roughy, wash fish and pat dry with paper towels. Sprinkle fish with 1½ tablespoons Seasoning Mix. Set aside. Combine milk and egg yolk in shallow dish. Combine flour and remaining 1½ tablespoons Seasoning Mix. Dredge fish in flour mixture, and dip in milk mixture. Dredge again in flour mixture. Pour oil to a depth of ¼-inch in an electric skillet, and heat to 350 degrees. Fry fish 2 to 3 minutes on each side. Drain well and keep warm. Spoon Brown Butter Sauce onto serving platter. Place fish on sauce, and spread each fillet with warm Pecan Butter Sauce. Serve immediately. Serves 6.

ORANGE ROUGHY SOUTHWESTERN STYLE

2 pounds orange roughy
  fillets
¾ cup sour cream
½ cup cream cheese, softened
1 cup shredded white
  Cheddar cheese
1 tablespoon onion, minced

1 tablespoon fresh lemon
  juice
½ teaspoon garlic salt
cayenne pepper to taste
1 4-ounce can diced green
  chilies
fresh cilantro, minced
paprika

Cut fish into serving pieces and place in single layer in an oiled baking dish. Blend sour cream and cream cheese until smooth. Add Cheddar cheese, onion, lemon juice, garlic salt, cayenne and chilies and mix well. Spread over fish. Bake at 375 degrees for 10 to 15 minutes, or until fish flakes easily. Garnish with cilantro and paprika. Red snapper, flounder or other white fish can be substituted for orange roughy. Serves 4-6.

CREOLE STYLE FLOUNDER

1 cup green onions, sliced
  with tops
1 large green pepper, sliced
  into thin strips
1½ tablespoons margarine,
  melted
1 16-ounce can whole
  tomatoes, undrained
1 8-ounce can tomato sauce

1 bay leaf
½ teaspoon dried whole
  thyme
6 flounder fillets
vegetable cooking spray
¼ teaspoon lite salt
⅛ teaspoon pepper
3 cups hot cooked rice

Sauté green onions and green pepper in margarine until tender. Add liquid from tomatoes. Stir in tomato sauce, bay leaf and thyme. Bring to a boil. Reduce heat and simmer, uncovered, for 20 minutes; remove bay leaf. Place fish in a 13 x 9 x 2-inch baking dish which has been coated with cooking spray; sprinkle fish with salt and pepper. Spoon sauce over fish; cover and bake at 350 degrees for 20 minutes, or until fish flakes when tested with fork. Serve over rice. Serves 6.

BAKED FISH ALMONDINE

14 saltine crackers, finely crushed
1½ teaspoons fresh lemon juice
butter or margarine
¼ teaspoon salt
2 tablespoons hot water
4 4-ounce portions fish, fresh or frozen (thaw slightly)
¼ cup mayonnaise
1½ tablespoons slivered almonds (or more, to taste)

Preheat oven to 400 degrees. Crush crackers between two sheets of wax paper, in a plastic bag, or process in food processor. Place lemon juice, 1½ teaspoons butter or margarine, salt and hot water in a small saucepan. Heat to boiling. Pour mixture into shallow baking dish that is large enough to hold fish. Place fish in lemon butter mixture in dish. Spread mayonnaise evenly about ¼-inch thick on top of fish. Melt 3 tablespoons butter or margarine in saucepan or microwave. Add crushed crackers and almonds to melted butter and combine. Sprinkle cracker mixture evenly over top portion of fish. Bake at 400 degrees until done, about 8 minutes. Garnish with fresh parsley and lemon slices. Serves 4.

SEAFOOD CASSEROLE

1 package frozen lobster tails (3), shelled
1 pound fresh shrimp, shelled and deveined
1 package fresh crab meat, cartilage removed
1 teaspoon onion, grated
½ cup butter
2½ cups medium white sauce (see Sauces)
1 heaping teaspoon dry mustard
1 tablespoon Worcestershire sauce
1 tablespoon onion, minced
2 dashes Tabasco
4 tablespoons white wine
salt and pepper to taste
buttered crumbs

Sauté the lobster, shrimp, crab meat and onion in the butter. In saucepan, heat white sauce and whisk in dry mustard, Worcestershire, onion, Tabasco, white wine, salt and pepper. Fold in prepared seafood and place in lightly oiled 2-quart casserole. Top with buttered crumbs. Cook 30 minutes at 350 degrees. Delicious served in puff pastry shells. Serves 6.

Soups and Sandwiches

Tyler Farmers' Market

The pavilions of the East Texas State Fairgrounds seem to burst with delectable fruits, vegetables, jams and jellies!

Beginning in May, farmers throughout East Texas bring their produce to sell on Tuesday, Thursday and Saturday. The cornucopia of garden foods available is as fresh as you can get and the quality is unsurpassed!

During the season, which extends through August, the market sponsors a vegetable and craft show. Sharing gardening techniques, tips for canning and family recipes – shopping has never been more fun!

GAZPACHO

4 medium tomatoes
1 cucumber
½ green pepper
2 cloves garlic

1 bunch green onions
1 teaspoon salt
½ teaspoon pepper

Dressing:
2 tablespoons olive oil
2 tablespoons red wine
    vinegar

½ cup ice cold water

Peel, seed and cut up tomatoes. Peel and seed cucumber. Cut green pepper in half and remove seeds and white membrane. Cut into chunks. Crush or mince garlic. Cut onions, with some green included, into small pieces. Put into a blender. Add salt and pepper. Pour dressing into the blender and turn blender on high and blend until everything is chopped finely but not liquefied. Can be served immediately or put into refrigerator for 2 to 3 hours until ready to serve. Serves 4.

CHILLED CUCUMBER SOUP

4 medium cucumbers, peeled
    and seeded
1 quart buttermilk
3 tablespoons green onions
salt to taste

8 large beefsteak tomatoes,
    chilled
lettuce leaves
3 cherry tomatoes, sliced thin
mint leaves

Chop cucumbers and put into blender with onions, buttermilk and salt. Puree until smooth. Pour into glass container, cover, and chill in refrigerator 4 to 6 hours. Shortly before serving, hollow out tomatoes and set pulp aside for another use. Place lettuce leaves on 8 serving plates. Spoon soup into tomatoes and center on lettuce. Garnish with cherry tomato slices and mint leaves. Serves 8.

MARA'S TACO SOUP

2 pounds lean ground beef
1 onion, chopped
1 package Original Hidden
   Valley Ranch Dressing
   mix
1 package taco seasoning
garlic powder to taste
1 can jalapeño pintos,
   undrained

1 can kidney beans,
   undrained
1 can golden hominy,
   undrained
1 can Rotel tomatoes,
   undrained
2 cans stewed tomatoes,
   undrained

Brown ground beef and chopped onion. Add 1 package Original Hidden Valley Ranch Dressing mix and 1 package taco seasoning. Add garlic powder to taste. Add undrained remaining ingredients. Simmer 45 minutes and enjoy! It's even better 3 days later!

TORTILLA SOUP

10 cups chicken stock
1 28-ounce can diced
   tomatoes
1 46-ounce can tomato juice
2 tablespoons bouillon
   granules
6 ribs celery, chopped
1 medium bell pepper,
   chopped
2 medium onions, chopped
   finely

4 cloves garlic, minced
3 tablespoons cumin
1 teaspoon chili powder
12 corn tortillas, cut up
3 cups cooked chicken meat,
   chopped (reserve liquid)
2 cups cooked rice
2 tablespoons chopped
   cilantro
pinch cayenne pepper
salt to taste

Combine and heat chicken stock, diced tomatoes, tomato juice and bouillon. Then add celery, bell pepper, onions, garlic, cumin and chili powder. Cook and simmer about 10 minutes. Add tortillas and let cook down, stirring occasionally. They will dissolve and thicken soup. Add chopped chicken and cooked rice. Stir to mix and cook about 5 more minutes. Add chopped cilantro, cayenne pepper and salt to taste. Serve hot with tortilla chips as garnish. Can be garnished with cubed avocado, if desired. **Variation:** Use 1 cup salsa and 1 8-ounce can tomato sauce instead of canned tomatoes and tomato juice. Serves 8.

CANNELLINI BEAN SOUP WITH GREENS

2 tablespoons extra virgin olive oil
1 large onion, minced
1 large garlic clove, chopped fine
1 small bunch spinach, turnip greens or Swiss chard, stemmed, washed and sliced into very thin shreds

6 cups chicken broth, preferably homemade, hot
1 12-ounce can rinsed, drained cannellini beans
¼ teaspoon salt or to taste
½ teaspoon freshly ground pepper
½ cup freshly grated Italian Parmesan cheese, preferably Parmigiana Reggiano

Heat olive oil in a 4-quart casserole or stock pot. Over medium heat cook onion and garlic until soft. Stir in greens, cook uncovered until wilted, add hot chicken broth and beans and cook 5 minutes. Season with salt and pepper, making it quite peppery. Serve hot with crusty country bread and Parmesan. Serves 4-6.

CHEESE SOUP

2 cups celery, chopped
½ cup green pepper, chopped
2 cans cream of mushroom soup
2 soup cans milk
½ cup tomato puree
¼ teaspoon coriander, ground

½ teaspoon white pepper
¼ cup sour cream
2 scant cups shredded Cheddar cheese
½ cup dry sherry
2 tablespoons parsley, chopped

Place 2 cups chopped celery and ½ chopped green pepper in water to cover. Cook until tender. Drain. Over low heat, blend 2 cans cream of mushroom soup with 2 soup cans milk. Puree the soup with vegetables in a blender (or pass through a fine sieve). Cook in a double boiler over hot (not boiling) water. Stirring, add ½ cup tomato puree, ¼ teaspoon ground coriander, ½ teaspoon white pepper, ¼ cup sour cream, 2 scant cups shredded Cheddar cheese, until the mixture is smooth and hot. Finish with ½ cup dry sherry and 2 tablespoons chopped parsley. If soup is too thick for your taste, thin with warm milk. Serve very hot. Serves 8.

CHEESY TOMATO SOUP

1 64-ounce can tomato juice
1 pound grated Cheddar
   cheese
16 ounces sour cream
1 small can Rotel tomatoes,
   pureed

In a large saucepan, heat all the ingredients. This is easy and very tasty.

DOUBLE CHEESE ONION SOUP

2 large onions, thinly sliced
¼ cup butter or margarine,
   melted
3 cups beef broth
2 cups chicken broth
2 cups water
½ cup sherry
2 cups French bread cubes,
   toasted
grated Parmesan cheese
7 slices mozzarella cheese

Separate onion into rings and sauté in butter in a large Dutch oven until tender. Add next 4 ingredients and bring to a boil. Reduce heat and simmer for 30 minutes. Remove from heat and stir in sherry. Add other ingredients to top of soup which is placed in oven-proof bowls. Put under broiler 6 inches from heat until cheese melts. Can be frozen. Yields 7 cups.

FRESH PEA SOUP WITH CROUTONS

3 tablespoons unsalted butter
2 cups fresh or frozen green
   peas
4 scallions, chopped
6 cups chicken stock or water
salt and pepper to taste
6 leaves fresh tarragon,
   finely chopped
croutons
heavy cream or crème fraîche

To make soup, melt butter in a pot, and add peas and scallions. Cook over medium-low heat for 5 minutes. Do not brown them. Add stock, bring to a boil. Reduce to a simmer, and cook until peas are tender, 10 to 15 minutes. Puree the soup in a blender or food processor. Season with salt and pepper, and add tarragon. Serve hot or cold with croutons. To make croutons, sauté ½-inch cubes of French bread in olive oil until brown and crispy. The soup can be enriched with a few tablespoons of heavy cream or crème fraîche, if you wish. Serves 4.

PORTUGUESE SOUP

1 cup onion, chopped
3 cloves garlic, chopped
3 tablespoons oil
½ pound garlic-flavored pork
  sausage (Elgin type or
  Linguica)
5 cups beef stock
1 cup cooked kidney beans,
  undrained

½ head green cabbage,
  chopped into medium
  pieces
6 small new potatoes,
  scrubbed and quartered
2 to 4 tablespoons vinegar
1 cup catsup
salt and pepper to taste

The chef/owner of the Inn at Brushy Creek at Round Rock, Texas, (no longer in existence) shared this wonderful recipe. Using a 3-quart saucepan, sauté onion and garlic in oil until just transparent. Cut sausage into bite-sized pieces; add to vegetables and brown lightly. Add beef stock and remaining ingredients. Bring soup to a boil, stirring frequently. Reduce heat and simmer 35 to 45 minutes, stirring occasionally. Correct seasonings to taste. The flavor of the soup is best when refrigerated for a few days and reheated. It will keep for 4 to 5 days refrigerated. Serves 8.

CREAM ZUCCHINI SOUP

2 tablespoons butter
½ cup sliced scallions
6 medium zucchini, thinly
  sliced
2 13¾-ounce cans chicken
  stock
2 tablespoons dry sherry

⅛ teaspoon pepper
⅛ teaspoon salt
dash nutmeg
1 cup light cream
3 tablespoons fresh Parmesan
  cheese, grated

In a large saucepan, melt the butter. Sauté scallions until softened. Add the zucchini and chicken broth and bring to a boil. Lower heat and simmer 8 to 10 minutes, until zucchini is tender. Allow to cool 15 minutes. In blender or food processor, process cooled zucchini mixture in small batches until smooth. Return to pan and stir in sherry, pepper, salt and nutmeg. Bring to a boil and remove from heat. Stir in cream and cheese. Serve hot or cover and chill in refrigerator 3 to 4 hours. Serves 8.

SOUP IN A PUMPKIN

1 6- to 7-pound pumpkin
2½ to 3 cups white
    homemade bread crumbs
2 cups minced onion
8 tablespoons butter
1½ cups grated Swiss cheese

2 quarts chicken broth,
    heated
salt, pepper and sage to taste
1 cup heavy cream
fresh parsley, chopped

Cut off top of pumpkin carefully. Save for a cover. Scrape out seeds and stringy part. Rub the pumpkin with butter, inside and out. Make bread crumbs in food processor, using day old bread. Place crumbs in 350 degree oven for 15 minutes to brown. Remove and set aside. Melt butter and slowly sauté onion until tender. Add bread crumbs and cook 3 minutes. Pour onion and crumb mixture into pumpkin. Stir in Swiss cheese. Fill to within 2 inches of top with hot chicken broth. Season with salt, pepper and ½ teaspoon sage. Bake on a pan with a lip in a 400 degree oven for 1½ hours. Do not overcook or pumpkin will collapse. Keep warm in 175 degree oven. Just before serving, add and stir in 1 cup heavy cream and freshly chopped parsley. Serves 10-12.

CHUNKY CHEESE CHOWDER

3 cups potatoes, chopped
1 cup carrots, chopped
1 cup celery, chopped
1 large onion, chopped
½ cup margarine
4 cups chicken broth

3 cups half and half
    (or 1 per cent milk for
    lower fat content)
¾ cup flour
1 pound Cheddar cheese,
    shredded
1 tablespoon parsley,
    chopped

In a 5-quart Dutch oven, cook vegetables in margarine until tender but not brown. Add broth, cover and cook 30 minutes. Blend half and half with flour and add to mixture. Add cheese and stir. Cook over low heat until thickened and heated through (do not boil). Sprinkle with parsley before serving. Freezes well. Serves 10.

KEY WEST CHOWDER

1 bunch green onions,
   chopped
1 cup butter
1 cup flour
1 pint half and half
2 cups celery, diced
2 cups carrots, sliced

4 cups water
4 tablespoons chicken
   bouillon
1 teaspoon seafood seasoning
1 pound seafood of your
   choice, cooked and diced
parsley for garnish

Sauté onions in butter. Add flour and stir 2 minutes over medium heat. Gradually add half and half, stirring another 2 minutes. Set aside. Bring carrots and celery to a boil in water and add bouillon. Cook until tender. Add cream mixture and seasoning. Add seafood last and do not overcook as it will toughen. Heat through. Garnish with parsley. Serves 6-8.

SWISS POTATO SOUP

2 tablespoons low fat
   margarine
1 onion, chopped
½ cup carrot, coarsely
   shredded
3 cups low fat milk
1 cup low sodium chicken
   broth

½ teaspoon salt
grated nutmeg to taste
¼ teaspoon black pepper
1 cup instant mashed potato
   flakes
½ cup Swiss cheese, shredded

Melt butter and add onion and carrot. Sauté 5 minutes or until tender. Stir in milk, broth, salt, nutmeg and pepper; bring to a boil. Stir in potato flakes until slightly thickened, about 1 minute. Add Swiss cheese and cook and stir until just melted. Serves 4.

DRESSING FOR MUFFALATTA SANDWICH

⅔ cup pitted green olives, chopped
⅔ cup pitted black olives, chopped
½ cup pimento, chopped
3 cloves garlic, finely chopped
1 anchovy fillet, mashed
1 tablespoon oregano

¼ teaspoon black pepper
½ cup olive oil
1 teaspoon lemon juice
1 tablespoon capers
⅓ cup parsley, chopped
¼ cup vinegar
1 onion, thinly sliced (optional)

Mix all ingredients, cover, and let marinate at least 12 hours. Yields enough for 1 large sandwich of Italian bread. If using as dressing on a salad, add finely chopped celery and thinly sliced carrots.

HOT CHICKEN SANDWICHES

16 slices very thin white bread
½ cup butter or margarine
¼ pound fresh mushrooms, sliced
2 tablespoons onions, finely minced
2 tablespoons butter or margarine
2 cups cooked chicken, cut into bite-sized pieces

3 hard-boiled eggs, chopped
⅓ cup black olives, drained and sliced
¾ cup mayonnaise (not salad dressing)
1 10¾-ounce can cream of chicken soup
1 cup sour cream
2 tablespoons cream sherry
paprika

Cut crust off bread. Spread ½ cup butter on both sides of each slice of bread. Place 8 of the 16 slices of bread in a 9 x 13-inch baking dish that has been sprayed with a non-stick cooking spray. In a large saucepan, sauté the mushrooms and onions in the remaining butter until mushrooms are lightly browned. Remove from heat. Stir in chicken, eggs, olives and mayonnaise, mixing well. Spread on top of bread in baking dish. Top with remaining 8 slices of bread. In a medium bowl, combine soup, sour cream, cream sherry and paprika. Pour over chicken sandwiches in baking dish. Bake in a preheated 325 degree oven for 30 minutes or until thoroughly heated. Cut into squares to serve. Makes 8 servings.

MY SISTER'S CHEESE PIMENTO

2 pounds sharp Cheddar
    cheese
2 large jars pimento, chopped
1 small onion, grated
2 heaping tablespoons
    prepared mustard

1 pint mayonnaise
2 teaspoons salt
2 tablespoons Worcestershire
    sauce

Mix all the ingredients and refrigerate. Spread on sandwiches or crackers.

CUCUMBER SANDWICHES

2 to 3 loaves Pepperidge
    Farm white bread, crusts
    removed

8 to 10 fresh small (not fat)
    cucumbers

Herb Mayonnaise:
1 cup mayonnaise
1 tablespoon vinegar
¼ teaspoon salt
¼ teaspoon paprika
⅛ teaspoon curry powder
1 tablespoon grated onion
¼ teaspoon garlic salt, or 1
    clove garlic, minced

1 tablespoon fresh chives,
    chopped
½ teaspoon Worcestershire
    sauce
1 teaspoon parsley
1 teaspoon oregano
1 teaspoon thyme
1 teaspoon basil
1 teaspoon dill

Mix ingredients for Herb Mayonnaise and store 1 day ahead. Slice cucumbers thinly and store in iced water in refrigerator. Spread crustless bread slices with Herb Mayonnaise to make sandwich. Store these in layers in a covered container in refrigerator, using damp tea towels to separate. On serving day, drain cucumbers VERY well. Dry with a paper towel if necessary. Place cucumber slices between bread slices. Slice into halves or quarters with a sharp bread knife. Layer between dampened towels to store or transport. Yields 80 small ¼ sandwiches.

Vegetables

Athens Black-Eyed Pea Jamboree

There couldn't be a better place to celebrate this tasty lentil than in Athens, the Black-Eyed Pea capital of the world. Every July, Athenians welcome thousands of visitors.

Festivities begin with a Pea-raid followed by the famous Black-Eyed Pea Cook-Off! There's also Pea-Eatin' and Pea-Smellin', arts and crafts, square dancing, carnival, gospel music, bass tournament, fun runs, the Miss Black-Eyed Pea Pageant and lots of good food everywhere.

In East Texas our tradition is to serve black-eyed peas on New Year's Day. As we savor the delicious legumes, we eagerly anticipate our good fortune for the coming year.

ARTICHOKES AND GREEN BEANS ROMANO

⅔ cup onion, finely chopped
1 clove garlic, minced
¼ cup olive oil
½ cup Italian bread crumbs
1 10-ounce package frozen
French-style green beans,
cooked and drained

1 14-ounce can artichoke
hearts, drained and
quartered
½ cup freshly grated Romano
cheese
salt and freshly ground
pepper to taste

In large skillet, sauté onion and garlic in olive oil until transparent. Stir in bread crumbs, blending well to absorb oil. Add green beans, artichoke hearts, and cheese. Combine thoroughly, yet gently. Heat slowly to soften cheese. Season to taste with salt and pepper. Serves 4.

ASPARAGUS PECAN BAKE

1 15-ounce cans asparagus
spears (reserve liquid),
or 2 pounds very thin
fresh asparagus, steamed
1 10¾-ounce can cream of
celery soup (mixed with
⅓ cup reserved liquid

1 5-ounce can sliced water
chestnuts
½ cup chopped pecans, toasted
2 cups Velveeta cheese, grated,
or for milder taste, 2 cups
grated Gouda cheese
salt and white pepper to taste

Preheat oven to 350 degrees. In an oven-proof dish, layer ½ the asparagus, ½ the soup, ½ water chestnuts, ½ pecans, ½ cheese. Repeat. Bake for 20 minutes, uncovered. Serves 6-8.

MAMA'S LIMAS

4 1-pound cans butter or lima
beans
¾ cup butter, melted
1 cup sour cream

1 cup brown sugar
1 tablespoon molasses
1 teaspoon dry mustard
salt to taste

Preheat oven to 300 degrees. Drain beans. Add remaining ingredients. Turn into 3-quart casserole. Bake, stirring occasionally. Recipe cannot be frozen, but can be made ahead and reheated. Serves 8 but can be halved easily.

MARGARET'S BAKED BEANS

2 cans jalapeño pinto beans
2 cans pork and beans
⅔ cup brown sugar
⅔ cup Woody's Cook-In
   sauce, or a barbecue
   concentrate

½ cup water
2 pounds lean ground beef
1 onion, chopped

Brown ground beef with onion. Drain. Mix all ingredients with beef and onion and put in a slow cooker on high for 4 to 5 hours, or in a 200 degree oven for 4 hours. Serves 8-10.

SUPPER BEANS

2 46-ounce cans pork and
   beans
½ cup hickory barbecue
   sauce
½ cup molasses
1 pound can crushed
   pineapple, undrained

½ box dark brown sugar
4 medium onions, chopped
3 green peppers, chopped
1 tablespoon dried mustard
1 14-ounce bottle catsup
¼ pound bacon, cooked,
   drained and crumbled

Mix ingredients. Bake in glass casserole dishes which have been sprayed with a vegetable baking spray. The longer and slower the baking the better. Bake 3 to 4 hours at 325 degrees, or cook in a slow cooker overnight on low. Serves 40.

GREEN BEANS WITH HERBS

2 pounds fresh green beans
1 cup water
¼ cup butter or margarine
2 teaspoons chopped chives
½ teaspoon sugar

¾ teaspoon salt
½ to 1 teaspoon dried whole
   tarragon
⅛ teaspoon pepper

Remove strings from beans; wash and cut into 1½-inch pieces. Combine beans and remaining ingredients in a large saucepan. Cover and cook over low heat 12 minutes or until crisp-tender. Serves 8.

BROCCOLI CASSEROLE

1 large onion, chopped
4 tablespoons margarine
1 can mushroom soup
1 roll garlic cheese, cubed
1 small can mushrooms,
  drained

½ cup almonds, blanched and
  toasted
2 packages frozen chopped
  broccoli, cooked and
  drained
½ cup bread crumbs

Preheat oven to 350 degrees. Sauté onion in margarine. Add mushroom soup, cubed garlic cheese, can of mushrooms, almonds and broccoli (cooked and drained). Place in casserole, top with bread crumbs, and heat until bubbly and golden on top, approximately 20 minutes. Serves 8.

BROCCOLI SUPREME

20 ounces slightly thawed
  frozen chopped broccoli
1 egg, beaten
1 pound can creamed corn
3 tablespoons grated onion

¼ teaspoon salt
¼ teaspoon pepper
6 tablespoons butter
2 cups Pepperidge Farm Herb
  Stuffing mix

Preheat oven to 350 degrees. Combine first 6 ingredients. Melt butter and toss with stuffing mix. Stir ¾ of stuffing mix into vegetables. Pour into greased 2-quart casserole. Sprinkle with remaining stuffing crumbs. Bake 40 minutes. Can be frozen. Serves 8-10.

SWEET AND SOUR CABBAGE

2 tablespoons vinegar
2 tablespoons water
1 tablespoon sugar (or more
  to taste)
1 to 2 teaspoons soy sauce

½ teaspoon salt
¼ cup oil
1 small cabbage, cut into
  ¼-inch strips
chow mein noodles

Combine vinegar, water, sugar, soy sauce and salt in small bowl. Set aside. Heat oil in heavy medium skillet over medium-high heat. Add cabbage and stir-fry until crisp-tender. Stir in vinegar mixture and toss quickly. Remove and serve crisp. Top with chow mein noodles. Serve immediately. Serves 4-6.

SWEET AND HOT BLACK EYED PEAS

1 pound dried black eyed
   peas, soaked overnight,
   drained
4 tablespoons unsalted
   butter, at room
   temperature
5 tablespoons water
2 medium onions, diced

2 red bell peppers, seeded
   and diced
2 green bell peppers, seeded
   and diced
2 cloves garlic, minced
1 small jalapeño chili, seeded
   and minced
½ teaspoon cayenne pepper
salt and black pepper to taste

Cover peas with fresh water. Bring to a boil; cover and lower heat. Simmer until tender, 30 minutes. Drain peas, reserving 1 cup liquid. Heat butter with water in saucepan. Add onions, bell peppers, garlic and jalapeño, and cook until softened. Season with cayenne, salt and black pepper. Add cooked peas with reserved cooking liquid and simmer until heated completely. Serves 8.

SOUTHWESTERN SOUFFLÉ

4 tablespoons butter
¼ cup flour
1 cup milk
¾ teaspoon salt
¼ teaspoon pepper
2 cups frozen corn, thawed
4 ounces Monterey Jack
   cheese (1 cup grated)

1 fresh or pickled jalapeño
   pepper, seeded and
   minced
4 scallions, sliced
⅓ cup chopped fresh cilantro
   (optional)
5 eggs, separated

Heat oven to 350 degrees. Butter and flour a 1½-quart soufflé dish. Melt butter in a saucepan. Add flour and cook over medium-low heat until it bubbles. Slowly stir in the milk and add salt and pepper. Boil, stirring constantly for 1 minute. Remove from heat and stir in corn, cheese, jalapeño pepper, scallions and cilantro. Separate eggs and beat in yolks. Cool. Beat egg whites until almost stiff. Fold ⅓ of the egg whites into corn mixture. Gently fold this lightened mixture into remaining whites. Pour into prepared dish and bake until risen and golden, about 45 minutes. Serve at once. Serves 4-6.

CARROT SOUFFLÉ (NEVER FAILS!)

2 cups carrots, cooked and
    whipped
½ cup butter, softened
½ cup sugar
3 eggs
¼ teaspoon cinnamon

1 tablespoon flour
1 teaspoon baking powder
1 teaspoon salt
1 cup milk
vegetable oil baking spray

Preheat oven to 350 degrees. Cream together butter and sugar. Add eggs one at a time, beating after each addition. Add carrots and beat. Add all other ingredients and beat until smooth. Pour into a sprayed 2-quart casserole dish and bake for 45 minutes. Serves 8.

ORANGE CARROTS

2 pounds baby carrots
¼ cup butter, melted
¼ cup brown sugar
¼ cup orange juice
    concentrate

½ cup mandarin orange
    pieces
½ teaspoon salt

Boil carrots until tender. Drain. Combine remaining ingredients until well blended. Place carrots in buttered baking dish, and cover with sauce. Refrigerate overnight. Turn carrots to coat with sauce. Bring to room temperature. Bake for 20-25 minutes at 350 degrees and serve hot. A garnish of fresh Italian parsley is nice. Serves 4-6.

DILLED CARROTS

1 bunch carrots (scrape and
    slice into 3-inch sticks)
¼ cup finely chopped onion
¼ cup Green Goddess
    dressing
¼ cup Italian dressing

1 teaspoon dried parsley (or
    1 tablespoon fresh),
    chopped
½ teaspoon pepper
½ teaspoon sugar
1 tablespoon dried dill weed
¼ teaspoon salt

Cook carrot sticks just until done (should be crisp). Drain and cool. Combine remaining ingredients. Add carrots and marinate overnight or up to a week. Serve cold. Serves 6.

CORN GARDEN HARVEST

3 medium ears fresh corn
1 small yellow onion,
   chopped
¼ cup green pepper, chopped
1 medium zucchini, sliced
   ¼-inch thick

2 packets artificial sweetener
   or 1 tablespoon sugar
1 teaspoon dried whole basil
⅛ teaspoon pepper
1 medium tomato, seeded and
   chopped

Cut corn from cobs. Place in 1½-quart casserole. Add onion and green pepper. Cover with plastic wrap and microwave on high for 2 minutes. Add remaining ingredients, except tomatoes. Cover and microwave on high for 7-8 minutes, stirring once. Add tomato. Cover and microwave for 1½ to 2 minutes until thoroughly heated. Serves 4.

Athens, Texas' beautiful lakes offer outstanding recreational opportunities. Texas' Governor George W. Bush proudly says that his lake home there is his family's favorite getaway place.

CORN AND GREEN CHILE CASSEROLE

5 15-ounce cans whole kernel
   sweet corn, drained
2 8-ounce packages cream
   cheese

3 4-ounce cans chopped
   green chilies, drained
½ teaspoon garlic powder
salt and pepper to taste
1 cup crushed cracker crumbs

Preheat oven to 350 degrees. Melt cream cheese in microwave. Add seasonings and green chilies. Pour over drained corn. Butter 11 x 13-inch Pyrex dish and fill with mixture. Top with cracker crumbs and dot with butter. Bake 30 minutes. Can be frozen. Serves 12.

EGGPLANT CASSEROLE

2 eggplants
1 onion, chopped
½ cup celery, chopped
½ cup butter
1¼ cups milk

1 teaspoon sage
¼ cup sugar
2 cups any variety cheese,
   grated
salt and pepper to taste

Preheat oven to 450 degrees. Peel, slice and boil eggplants in salted water until tender. Drain and chop. Slightly sauté celery and onions in butter and mix remaining ingredients together, except cheese. Place in greased baking dish. Bake for 20 minutes. Top with cheese and return to oven to melt cheese. [**Variation:** Add ½ roll Owen's hot sausage (cooked and drained), 2 eggs, ½ cup milk, and pour into greased sheet cake pan. Cook until well set. Cut into small squares and serve as appetizers.]

FRIED GREEN TOMATOES OR EGGPLANT

6 green tomatoes
   (or eggplant) cut into
   ½-inch slices
1 cup flour, seasoned with
   lite salt, black pepper
   and dried basil to taste

3 tablespoons
   (approximately) canola
   oil

In an iron skillet, pour enough canola oil to barely cover bottom. Heat on high. Mix flour, salt, pepper and dried basil together in a pie pan. Wash and dry tomatoes (or eggplant). Slice and dredge in flour mixture. When oil is hot, gently place slices in skillet. Turn only once. Don't overcook; mushy fried green tomatoes are not SOUTHERN! Serve hot for wonderful childhood memories of the South. Serves 6.

1015 ONIONS

3 large onions, sliced thin
1 can cream of chicken soup

1 cup grated cheese
1 cup crushed potato chips

Slice onions into buttered casserole dish. Pour soup over. Cover with cheese and potato chips. Bake 45 minutes at 350 degrees.

NOONDAY ONION CASSEROLE

½ cup unsalted butter, room
temperature
4 large Noonday onions, or
other sweet onions,
sliced in ½-inch rings
1½ cups buttery flavored
crackers (6 ounces or 50
crackers), crushed

8 ounces Cheddar cheese,
shredded
salt to taste
paprika to taste
3 large eggs, beaten
1 cup milk

Preheat oven to 350 degrees. Sauté onion rings in ¼ cup butter.

Reserve ¼ of crumb mixture for topping. Combine remaining butter with cracker crumbs and layer into bottom of greased 9 x 13-inch casserole. Spread sauteed onion rings over crumb layer and sprinkle with cheese, salt and paprika. Combine eggs and milk and pour over layers. Top with reserved crumb mixture. Bake 35-40 minutes. Can be frozen. Can be made ahead and reheated. Serves 8.

ENGLISH PEA AND PIMENTO CASSEROLE

1 cup celery, chopped
½ cup bell pepper, chopped
¾ cup onion, chopped
4 tablespoons margarine
2 10-ounce packages frozen
English peas, thawed
and drained
1 10-ounce can cream of
mushroom soup

1 8-ounce can water
chestnuts, drained and
chopped
1 2-ounce jar diced pimentos,
undrained
2 tablespoons margarine,
melted
½ cup fine dry bread crumbs

Preheat oven to 350 degrees. Sauté celery, bell pepper and onion in margarine. Add peas, soup, water chestnuts and pimento. Put into an 8 x 12-inch baking dish. Combine margarine and bread crumbs. Sprinkle over casserole. Bake for 30 minutes. Serves 8.

SESAME SNOW PEAS

1 pound fresh snow peas
½ cup water
1 tablespoon light sesame oil
1 tablespoon sesame seeds,
    toasted

1 tablespoon lemon juice
¼ teaspoon white pepper
⅛ teaspoon salt

Trim ends and strings from snow peas. Place in water in a saucepan. Bring to full boil. Cover and reduce heat. Simmer 3-5 minutes or until crisp-tender. Drain. Plunge snow peas into cold water. Drain again and pat dry with paper towels. Heat sesame oil in large skillet. Add peas and cook on medium heat stirring constantly just until coated. Sprinkle with sesame seeds, lemon juice, pepper, and salt. Toss well. Serve immediately. Serves 6.

ROASTED RED PEPPERS

6 red sweet peppers,
    quartered lengthwise and
    seeded

2 tablespoons fresh lemon
    juice
1 teaspoon coarsely ground
    black pepper

Preheat broiler. Place quartered peppers skin side up on broiler pan. Broil the peppers 2 to 3 inches from the heat. Watch carefully, and when the skin blackens, turn the peppers and broil until skins are black all over. Remove from broiler and using tongs, transfer the peppers to a plastic bag and seal it well. Let the peppers steam in a bag for 15 to 20 minutes. Remove from the bag and peel off the skins. Place the peppers in a shallow dish, drizzle them with the lemon juice and sprinkle with black pepper. Chop and use as needed. Trade secret: Keep roasted and peeled peppers covered with a bit of olive oil in the refrigerator. Delicious tossed in pasta. Serves 6.

GARLIC POTATOES

2 pounds baking potatoes
2 garlic cloves, peeled and cut
　in half
¼ cup olive oil
⅔ teaspoon salt

¼ teaspoon freshly ground
　pepper
2 tablespoons fresh parsley,
　chopped
1 tablespoon fresh chives,
　chopped

Scrub potatoes and cut into long ½-inch wedges. Place potatoes in a large pot of boiling salted water. Cover and bring to a boil over high heat. Uncover and cook 5 minutes. Drain. Spread potatoes out on paper towels and let dry (recipe can be prepared to this point up to 8 hours ahead. Cover and refrigerate potatoes if this is done). Preheat oven to 325 degrees. Heat garlic in oil over low heat in small saucepan 10 to 15 minutes, until garlic begins to brown. Move potatoes to a shallow bowl and toss gently with garlic, salt and pepper. Transfer to a baking sheet and drizzle with remaining oil from saucepan. Bake for 45 minutes. Increase oven temperature to 425 degrees and bake, tossing once or twice until potatoes are browned and crisp, 15-20 minutes. Discard garlic cloves before serving. Serve with chopped parsley and chives. Serves 4-6.

POTATO CASSEROLE

1 2-pound package frozen
　hash browns, thawed
½ cup butter, melted
1 can cream of chicken soup

salt and pepper to taste
½ yellow onion, chopped
　finely
1 pint sour cream

Topping:
2 cups corn flakes, crushed　　¼ cup butter, melted

Preheat oven to 250 degrees. Spray a 10 x 13-inch Pyrex dish with a vegetable cooking spray. Place potatoes in a 3-quart bowl and mix with melted butter. Add remaining ingredients to potatoes and mix well. Turn into the prepared dish. Cover with corn flake topping and bake for 1 hour. Can be frozen, or made ahead and reheated. Serves 8-10.

OVEN-BROWNED POTATOES WITH PANCETTA (BACON) AND ROSEMARY

6 pounds medium new
potatoes, peeled
½ cup (1 stick) unsalted
butter, room temperature
6 slices thinly sliced pancetta
(Italian bacon), coarsely
chopped, or 6 slices
bacon, blanched and
chopped

½ cup light-bodied olive oil
2 tablespoons crumbled dried
rosemary, or 8 sprigs
fresh
1 teaspoon salt
⅛ teaspoon freshly ground
pepper
fresh parsley or rosemary
sprigs (garnish)

Place potatoes in deep large pot and cover with cold water. Bring to boil over high heat and cook until potatoes are still a bit firm when pierced with knife, about 15 to 20 minutes for medium potatoes. Do not overcook. Drain potatoes and let cool several minutes. Preheat oven to 450 degrees. Using all the butter, coat bottom and sides of shallow large baking pan (such as broiler pan). Cut potatoes into large chunks and add to pan. Sprinkle with bacon, olive oil, rosemary, salt and pepper, reserving garnish. (Potatoes can be prepared 1 day ahead up to this point. Bring to room temperature before recrisping at 400 degrees.) Roast, turning often, until all butter and oil are absorbed and potatoes are very crisp, about 1 to 1¼ hours. To serve, turn into shallow serving bowl and garnish with parsley or rosemary. Serves 8-10.

ASPARAGUS WITH CAPER DILL SAUCE

1 cup sour cream or yogurt
¼ cup fresh lemon juice
3 tablespoons fresh dill
¼ cup capers, drained
½ teaspoon salt

½ teaspoon freshly ground
pepper
1 pound fresh asparagus or
green beans, blanched

Blend all ingredients except asparagus or beans. Chill for one hour. Serve over blanched asparagus or green beans.

GARDEN VEGETABLE CASSEROLE

4 medium potatoes, peeled
   and sliced
2 onions, thinly sliced
1 medium zucchini, sliced
4 to 5 tomatoes, sliced and
   seeded

3 carrots, pared
1 cup Rhine wine
salt and pepper to taste
¼ cup butter, melted
1 cup bread crumbs
2 cups grated Cheddar cheese

Preheat oven to 375 degrees. Slice potatoes thinly and spread in medium sized ungreased casserole. Place onions, in rings, over potatoes. Layer zucchini over onions. Next layer tomatoes, then carrots (which have been sliced). Add salt and pepper to wine and pour over layered ingredients. Cover with foil and bake for one hour. Remove from oven. Mix bread crumbs with butter and spread over vegetables. Sprinkle grated cheese over all. Return to oven. Bake uncovered 15 minutes longer, but reduce temperature to 325 degrees. Can be frozen, or made ahead and reheated. Serves 8-10.

SWEET POTATO CASSEROLE

3 cups whipped sweet
   potatoes
1 cup sugar
¼ cup margarine

½ cup milk
½ teaspoon salt
2 eggs
1 teaspoon vanilla

Topping:
1 cup brown sugar
½ cup all purpose flour
¼ cup margarine, melted

1 cup chopped pecans,
   toasted

Preheat oven to 350 degrees. Combine first 7 ingredients and pour into a 9 x 13-inch sprayed baking dish. Mix topping ingredients and sprinkle over potatoes. Bake 30 minutes. Very good with turkey at Thanksgiving or Christmas. Serves 8.

SQUASH CASSEROLE

2 cups applesauce
¼ cup brown sugar
½ teaspoon salt
½ cup heavy cream
1¼ cups yellow crook neck
   squash, cooked drained
   and mashed (measured
   after cooking)

⅛ teaspoon nutmeg
6 tablespoons melted butter
   (divided use)
2 eggs, beaten
½ cup white bread crumbs
½ cup slivered almonds,
   toasted

Preheat oven to 375 degrees. Mix applesauce, brown sugar, salt, cream, squash, nutmeg, eggs, and 4 tablespoons of butter. Place in greased 1½-quart casserole. Mix crumbs, remaining 2 tablespoons of butter, and almonds. Sprinkle over squash mixture. Bake uncovered for 35 minutes. May be frozen. Serves 6-8.

TEXICAN SQUASH

2½ pounds yellow or zucchini
   squash, sliced
¾ cup water
4 eggs
½ cup milk
1 pound Monterey Jack
   cheese, grated
1 teaspoon salt

2 teaspoons baking powder
3 tablespoons flour
1 4-ounce can chopped green
   chilies
2 jalapeños, seeded and
   chopped (optional)
1¼ cups crushed tortilla chips
   or bread crumbs

Boil squash in water until barely tender. Drain and cool. Mix eggs, milk, cheese, salt, baking powder, flour, chilies and jalapeños together and fold into squash. Butter a 9 x 13-inch casserole and sprinkle bottom with crushed tortilla chips. Pour in squash mixture. Sprinkle top with more crushed chips or crumbs. Bake at 350 degrees for 30 minutes. Serves 8.

SQUASH DRESSING

2 pounds yellow squash
¼ cup water
1 6-ounce package cornbread
   mix, baked and crumbled
2 cups milk
½ cup celery, chopped
½ cup onion, chopped

2 tablespoons margarine
1 teaspoon black pepper
1 10-ounce can cream of
   chicken soup
2 teaspoons poultry
   seasoning

Mix, bake and crumble cornbread into bowl with milk in it. Set aside. Cook squash in water in covered pan until tender. Drain and mash. Preheat oven to 350 degrees. Sauté celery and onion in margarine until tender. Add pepper, soup, poultry seasoning, and squash. Stir into cornbread mixture. Pour into a greased 2-quart casserole. Bake for one hour until set at 350 degrees. Serves 8.

PRUFROCK BAKED SQUASH

1¾ pounds yellow crook neck
   squash
2 tablespoons butter or
   margarine, melted
1 cup dry bread crumbs,
   divided in half
1½ tablespoons sugar

½ teaspoon salt
1 tablespoon dehydrated
   onion flakes
fresh cracked black pepper to
   taste
2 eggs, beaten

Preheat oven to 350 degrees. Cut squash into 2-inch chunks. Boil squash, or microwave until just tender. Place squash in colander and drain as much water as possible from them. Let drain 10 minutes. In a mixing bowl, combine squash, butter, ½ cup bread crumbs, seasonings, and egg. Place in a lightly greased 2-quart casserole dish, and top with remaining bread crumbs. Bake covered at 350 degrees for 20 minutes, or until set. Remove cover and return to oven. Bake just until bread crumbs are lightly browned, about 10 minutes longer. Serves 6.

SPINACH ARTICHOKE BAKE

½ cup chopped green onion
  with tops
2 cloves garlic, finely minced
½ cup butter
4 cups frozen spinach,
  cooked, drained and
  salted
1 cup sour cream

¼ cup grated Parmesan
  cheese
2 tablespoons lemon juice
½ teaspoon tarragon flakes
1 can artichoke hearts,
  quartered
½ cup bread crumbs

Sauté onions and garlic in butter and add to drained spinach. Stir in sour cream, cheese, lemon juice, tarragon flakes and artichokes. Lightly spray 2-quart baking dish with cooking spray and add the mixture. Sprinkle with buttered bread crumbs and bake at 350 degrees for 30 minutes. Serves 8.

PARTY SPINACH

1 16-ounce package cut leaf
  spinach, cooked and
  well-drained (reserve ½
  cup liquid)
4 tablespoons butter or
  margarine
2 tablespoons flour
1 medium yellow onion,
  finely chopped

4 garlic cloves, finely
  chopped
½ cup cream, or half and half
½ teaspoon black pepper,
  freshly cracked
¾ teaspoon salt (or to taste)
½ to ¾ teaspoon Tabasco
1 6-ounce roll sharp cheese,
  cubed
1 small jar chopped pimento

Cook spinach according to package directions. DRAIN VERY WELL. Melt butter in pan over low heat. Add flour and blend until smooth, but not brown. Add onion and garlic and cook until soft. Stir in cream and reserved spinach liquid. Blend until slightly thickened. Add pepper, salt, pepper sauce, cubed cheese, and pimento. Combine with well drained spinach. Arrange in a 2-quart baking dish and bake 25 minutes at 350 degrees if using as a vegetable. If using as a dip, cook 20 minutes in skillet and transfer to a chafing dish to serve with toast or plain crackers. Serves 8.

SPINACH STUFFED TOMATOES

8 medium tomatoes with tops
  cut off and pulp removed
2 10-ounce packages frozen
  chopped spinach, cooked
  and drained
1 cup bread crumbs
1 cup Parmesan cheese,
  grated
3 green onions, chopped
2 eggs
3 tablespoons butter, melted
½ teaspoon thyme
½ teaspoon Accent
¼ teaspoon garlic powder

Cook spinach; **DRAIN WELL.** Combine with all remaining ingredients and spoon into tomatoes. Bake in shallow pan 30 minutes at 325 degrees. Serves 8.

JAMBOREE BLACKEYED PEA CASSEROLE

1 cup yellow cornmeal
½ cup flour
1 teaspoon salt
½ teaspoon soda
1 cup buttermilk
2 eggs
½ cup oil
1 cup chopped onion
1 cup cooked blackeyed peas
¾ cup creamed corn
1 pound ground meat,
  browned (or sausage)
½ pound Cheddar cheese,
  grated

Mix all ingredients except cheese. Pour into a greased 2-quart casserole dish. Add cheese last. Bake at 350 degrees for 45 minutes.

JIM'S ESCALLOPED TOMATOES

1 small onion, finely chopped
¼ cup butter
1¼ cups dry bread cubes (or
  plain croutons)
½ cup brown sugar
3½ cups canned, peeled
  tomatoes
1 teaspoon salt
⅛ teaspoon pepper

Sauté onion in butter using an iron frying pan. Add bread cubes and sugar. Cook slowly. Stir in tomatoes and seasonings. Place mixture in buttered shallow pan. Bake 45 minutes at 350 degrees.

TOMATOES FLORENTINE

12 plum tomatoes
2 ounces Swiss cheese
1 cup Progresso bread crumbs
10 ounces frozen spinach
4 tablespoons melted butter

Cut off tops of tomatoes; scoop out insides. Combine remaining ingredients and spoon into tomatoes. Bake at 350 degrees for 15 minutes.

SWEET BASIL BROILED TOMATOES

3 large firm tomatoes, halved
1 teaspoon sugar
½ teaspoon salt
½ teaspoon pepper
1½ teaspoons dried sweet basil
3 tablespoons butter, melted
1 clove garlic
3 tablespoons bread crumbs

Place tomato halves on 15 x 11 x 1-inch pan. Combine sugar, salt, pepper and sweet basil and sprinkle over tomato halves. Crush garlic into melted butter. Sauté for 2 minutes. Sprinkle bread crumbs over tomatoes, and 1½ teaspoons garlic/butter over each. Place under broiler, 4 to 5 inches from heat, until top browns (approximately 3-4 minutes). Serves 6.

WILD RICE WITH CURRANTS AND APPLES

1 cup wild rice, cooked and
   drained
1 cup brown rice, cooked and
   drained
1 cup dried currants
   (or raisins)
4 tablespoons chopped fresh
   parsley
3 tablespoons orange zest
1 Granny Smith apple, diced
2 tablespoons extra virgin
   olive oil
2 tablespoons freshly
   squeezed orange juice
salt and freshly ground
   pepper
fresh grated Parmesan cheese
fresh parsley for garnish

Preheat oven to 350 degrees. In mixing bowl, combine cooked rices. Gently toss currants, parsley, zest, apple, oil, orange juice, salt and pepper with combined rices. Place mixture in casserole, cover with foil, and heat thoroughly 20 minutes. Sprinkle with cheese and parsley. Serves 6-8.

DIRTY RICE

2 tablespoons oil
½ pound chicken gizzards, ground
¼ pound ground pork
2 bay leaves
2 tablespoons butter
½ cup chopped onions
½ cup chopped celery

½ cup chopped green bell pepper
2 tablespoons minced garlic
2 cups basic chicken stock
⅓ pound chicken livers, ground
¾ cup uncooked rice

Seasoning Mix:
2 tablespoons cayenne pepper
1½ teaspoons pepper
1¼ tablespoons paprika

1 tablespoon dry mustard
1 tablespoon cumin
½ teaspoon thyme leaves
½ teaspoon oregano

Combine ingredients for seasoning mix and set aside. Place oil, gizzards, pork and bay leaves in a heavy skillet over high heat. Cook until thoroughly browned, especially the pork. Add butter, onions, celery, bell pepper, and garlic. Stir. Reduce heat, stirring constantly to scrape bottom well. Add stock and stir until mixture is released from pan bottom. Add seasoning mix. Cook about 8 minutes over high heat. Stir in chicken livers and cook 2 minutes more. Add rice and stir thoroughly. Cover pan and turn heat to very low. Cook until rice is tender. Remove from heat and leave covered until rice is tender (about 10 minutes). Remove bay leaves and serve. Serves 6.

DELICIOUS ZUCCHINI PIE

1 8-ounce can refrigerator
  crescent rolls
⅓ cup salted cashews,
  chopped
2 tablespoons butter
2 to 3 medium zucchini, with
  peel, thinly sliced

1 onion, finely chopped
1 teaspoon dried dill
salt and pepper to taste
2 eggs lightly beaten
1 cup Monterey Jack cheese,
  cubed
chopped parsley

In a 9-inch pie plate, lay out rolls to form a pie crust. Place chopped cashews on the bottom of crust. In a skillet, melt butter and sauté zucchini and onion until translucent. Add dill, salt and pepper to taste. Pour mixture over nuts. Cover with beaten eggs. Top with the cheese and sprinkle with parsley. Bake in 325 degree oven for 40 minutes or until crust is lightly browned and eggs are set. Outstanding side dish. Serves 6-8.

DILLED ZUCCHINI

3 pounds zucchini, cubed
1 large yellow onion, minced
6 tablespoons butter
2 tablespoons flour
½ cup sour cream

⅓ cup lemon juice
1 teaspoon sugar
salt to taste
1 to 2 tablespoons dill weed

Cook zucchini in steamer until tender. Sauté onion in butter. Mix in flour and sour cream. Add lemon juice, sugar and salt. Stir. Add dill weed and zucchini. Mix. Pour into buttered casserole. Cover and bake at 325 degrees until bubbly, about 30 minutes. Serves 8.

ZUCCHINI AND TOMATOES IN CREAM SAUCE

3 medium zucchini, thinly
 sliced
8 small tomatoes, thinly
 sliced

1 medium onion, thinly sliced
½ cup fresh Parmesan cheese

Basil Cream Sauce:
3 tablespoons unsalted
 butter, melted
2 tablespoons all purpose
 flour
1 cup half and half

¼ cup fresh basil or 1
 tablespoon dried
1 teaspoon chicken granules
 (or bouillon cube)
fresh pepper and salt to taste

To make Basil Sauce, cook butter and flour over medium heat, stirring constantly for 2 minutes. Add half and half, basil, bouillon granules, salt and pepper. Stir until thickened, about 2-3 minutes. Remove from heat. Preheat oven to 350 degrees. Layer half the zucchini, tomatoes and onion in greased 9½ x 11-inch baking dish. Season each layer with salt and pepper. Sprinkle with half the Parmesan. Repeat layers and spoon cream sauce over the top. Sprinkle with remaining cheese. Bake uncovered for 45 minutes.

ZUCCHINI TORTE

2 pounds zucchini, 1 pound
 sliced and 1 pound
 grated
1 lemon rind, grated
4 eggs

¼ cup Parmesan cheese
½ cup bread crumbs (reserve
 half for topping)
salt and pepper to taste
butter

Preheat oven to 375 degrees. After washing zucchini, thinly slice 1 pound zucchini and coarsely grate the other pound into a small bowl. Grate lemon rind. In a second bowl mix eggs with Parmesan cheese. Add grated lemon rind, 4 tablespoons bread crumbs, salt and pepper. Combine zucchini and egg mixture and mix well. Butter a 10-inch pie plate and coat with bread crumbs. Add zucchini/egg mixture. Top with reserved bread crumbs and place in oven for 35 minutes. Cool and slice for serving. Serves 8.

NOTES

CONTRIBUTORS

Marilyn Abegg
Carole Jean Abernathy
Norine Acker
Annabel Adams
Marjorie Adams
Linda Alexander
Louree Alexander
Kathryn Allen
Alice Anderson
Barbara Anderson
Gwen Anderson
Rosemary Anderson
Patty Andrews
Kristi Armstrong
Charla Primer Autry
Carolyn Baer
Donna Barenkamp
Diane Barnes
Ann Basila
Paula Bates
Lisa Beaird
Jo Ann Belue
Rayline Binion
Evelyn Bochow
Sharlotte Bradley
Sue Bracco
Paula Breedlove
Dianna Brown
William J. Brown, M.D.
Marilyn Budde
Dottie Buie
Barbara Burleson
Cathy Bussey
Eleanor Cameron
Patsy Campbell
Virginia Chambers
Sharon Clark
Becky Colip
Dot Cornelius
Norman Cotten
Susan Cotten
Norma Cotton
Janet Cram
Elizabeth Cromer
Karen Crosby
Mary Jane Culver
Kevin A. Curran, M.D.

Mark A. D'Andrea, M.D.
Clay Davidson
Judy Davis
Mary Dawson
Cathy Dean
Margarita de la Garza-
    Grahm, M.D.
Mary De Lamar
Karen Dick
Mary Dodge
Susan Donaldson
Teresa Dreyfuss
Pat Farrington
Alicia Hudnall Fanning
Maytee Fisch
Rusty Fletcher
Carol Foox
Donna Freeman
Mayra Gallardo
Rafael L. Gallardo, M.D.
Marge Gelderman
Mary Lynn Gilpin
Mrs. Jesse Goldfeder
Louise Goss
Kay Gribble
Nancy Gross
Nez Gross
Jane Guillebeau
Martha Jennie Guinn
Carole Haberle
Judy Hagler
Carolyn Hammett
Betty Hargrave
Jean Harris
Marsha Harrison
Ruth Harrison
Helen Haycraft
Doris Haygood
Carole Hawkins
Glenda Heaton
Zelda Hightower
June Hillis
Margaret Hillyer
Susan Hood
Joyce Hudnall
John Franklin Hudnall,
    M.D.

Robin Clark Hudnall
Jana Humphrey
Jesmarie Hurst
Judy Hurst
Judith Isaacson
Helen Israel
Louella Jennings
Julie Johnson
Mary Johnston
Anita Jones
Terri Joseph
Kirt Kibbee
Cindy Kidwell
Ethel Kimmell
Phyllis Kimmell
Janie King
Ethel Knarr
Cathy Primer Krafve
Carole Kronenberg
Ali Langsjoen
Carol Langsjoen
Dorothy Lawrence
Dale Lawson
Bonnie Lee
Elizabeth Le Sauvage
Joan Le Sauvage
Katie Le Sauvage
Polly Lewis
Joy Lockhart
Vada Lockhart
Jo Lowery
Marilyn Luckett
Debbie Lundy
Jean Lyles
Kathie Mack
Andrea Madar
Zana Martin
James McBurney, M.D.
Sue McBurney
Teresa McCarty
Junella McClusky
Janet McKinley
Carolyn Means
Mary Meyers
Suzy Mighell
Peggy Morrow
Mother Francis Hospital

Sally Mullowney
Evelyn Muntz
John Nelson, M.D.
Sharon Nelson
Elizabeth Newbury
Dinah Noble
Frances Norton
Jan Norton
Jo Ann Norton
Karen Norton
Allene Odum
Alice Parrish
Kay Parrish
Joan Palmisano
Penny Patterson
Deborah Payne
Joyce Perry
Linda Pesnell
Pat Pinkenberg
Deborah Pitts
Ann Primer
Sandie Propst
Mary Prud'homme
Deborah Race
Toni Reardon
Retha Reece
Rhonda Reuter
Sandra Richert
Janet Rippy
Suzie Thomas Rippy
Hannah Robert
Joey Roberts

Steven B. Roberts, M.D.
Marianne Roberts
Anne Robertson
Betty Robinson
David L. Robinson, M.D.
Pam Roche
Francis Rogers
Jeanie Rogers
Virginia Rounds
Lori Rudak
Peggy Ryder
Helena Schnautz
Sally Schnautz
Barbara Schreiber
Kay Scroggins
Cris Selman
Marilyn Serber
Marie Louise Shaw
Sue Shaw
Johnnie Shepard
Lynn Short
Jill Sigal
Stephen Sigal, M.D.
Lois Silkman
Adlyn Smith
Ann Smith
Betty Ann Smith
Lori Smith
Mary Gean Smyth
Elizabeth Snider
Kathy Spivey
Melinda Stanley

Marie Starling
Sandy Stewart
Rena Stiefel
Carolyn Stitt
Jan Stock
Eleanor Stringer
Mary Dale Thomas
Debbie Townsend
Gloria Townsend
Leslie Triggs
Laura Turner
Mary Turner
Beulah Tuttle
Mary Lou Tyer
Serena Vrnak
Claudia Waldron
Martha Walker
Beverly Weitzman
Mrs. Thomas Wertz
Tickie West
Lynne Whatley
Gail White
D'Anna Wick
Corky Willens
Lewis Williams
Tracy Williams
Melody Wilson
Rhonda Womble
Ann Woods
Nancy Wrenn
Nancy Wright

NOTES

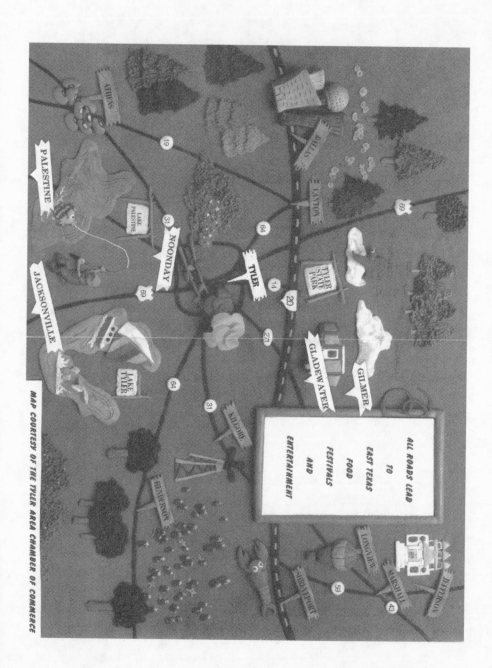

INDEX

INDEX

Smith County Medical Society Alliance
P.O. Box 7491
Tyler, Texas 75711

Please send ____ copy(ies) of *Azaleas to Zucchini* @ $15.95 each _____
Postage and handling @ 2.75 each _____
Texas residents add sales tax @ 1.24 each _____
TOTAL *19.94*

Name _____

Address _____

City _____ State _____ Zip _____

Make checks payable to Smith County Medical Society Alliance

- -

Smith County Medical Society Alliance
P.O. Box 7491
Tyler, Texas 75711

Please send ____ copy(ies) of *Azaleas to Zucchini* @ $15.95 each _____
Postage and handling @ 2.75 each _____
Texas residents add sales tax @ 1.24 each _____
TOTAL _____

Name _____

Address _____

City _____ State _____ Zip _____

Make checks payable to Smith County Medical Society Alliance

- -

Smith County Medical Society Alliance
P.O. Box 7491
Tyler, Texas 75711

Please send ____ copy(ies) of *Azaleas to Zucchini* @ $15.95 each _____
Postage and handling @ 2.75 each _____
Texas residents add sales tax @ 1.24 each _____
TOTAL _____

Name _____

Address _____

City _____ State _____ Zip _____

Make checks payable to Smith County Medical Society Alliance